11    $4 00 P   C0-ATH-594

DISCARDED

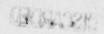

BYRON AND
THE SPOILER'S ART

BYRON
And the Spoiler's Art

PAUL WEST

CARL A. RUDISILL LIBRARY
LENOIR RHYNE COLLEGE

1960

ST MARTIN'S PRESS

NEW YORK

Copyright © Paul West 1960
Library of Congress Catalog Card Number: 60-11891

821.7
W52b

42,597.
March, 1962

To

PAULA

. . . that seeming marble heart,
Now mask'd in silence or withheld by pride,
Was not unskilful in the spoiler's art,
And spread its snares licentious far and wide . . . .

Childe Harold II, xxxiii, 1812

To withdraw *myself* from *myself* (oh that
cursed selfishness!) has ever been my sole,
my entire, my sincere motive in scribbling at
all; and publishing is also the continuance
of the same object, by the action it affords
to the mind, which else recoils upon itself.

(*Journal* of 1813)

CONTENTS

AUTHOR'S NOTE

THIS book is an attempt to regard Byron's poetry as something more than biographical evidence. I have aimed at a study which detains the reader only long enough to tempt him – if at all – to the poetry; a study, not monumental yet not quite invisible if seen sideways, suggesting the poet's quality, variety and present-day relevance.

I wish to thank the Canada Council, under whose patronage most of the writing was undertaken, as well as the editors of *The Bulletin of the Keats-Shelley Association, Dalhousie Review, Essays in Criticism* and *The Twentieth Century*, in which versions of parts of this study appeared. Finally, my thanks to Dr E. R. Seary for encouraging me to begin, and to the several very patient people who let me try out on them portions of the manuscript and long stretches of Byron himself.

P.W.

Chapter 1

POET IN PERSON

That man never wrote from his heart. He got up rapture and
enthusiasm with an eye to the public.

(THACKERAY on Byron)

THE pageant of the bleeding heart has run dry, and Mr Leslie
Marchand's monumental three-volume biography has, one
fondly hopes, entombed the surfeit. For it has been customary
to regard Byron's poetry as a useful and rather tedious index to
his personality. His various and exotic *personæ* have supplied
biographers with sustaining images and extravagant postures.
His satirical poems have received a nod of exemption, for they
give least scope to imaginative biographers who, confronted
with Lara, Manfred, the Childe, the Corsair and the other
personæ, can always justify their re-creations by adducing his
inconsistency of character. Inconsistent he certainly was; by
fits, turns and permutations, also sensitive, hard-boiled, shy,
supercilious; indolent and industrious, euphoric and morbid,
gross and fastidious, quixotic and self-centred, romantic and
unspiritual, feminine and brave, vindictive and generous – the
catalogue evinces but cannot exhaust or explain him. It would,
no doubt, be possible to list his predominant traits and to
demonstrate that within the limits of each he was consistent in
his own fashion. But such an exercise would be retrograde and
possibly repetitive: it would turn attention once again to the
Byronic *agon*, which is already over-documented, at the expense
of a fresh approach, which is to look at the man for the sake of
the writings.

Such an approach seems to have begun already. Mr Auden in
a broadcast Oxford lecture has drawn attention to the comic
skill of *Don Juan*; Mr W. W. Robson has written on Byron's

seriousness and complex sincerity; and M. Robert Escarpit, in his two-volume study of 'un tempérament littéraire', has studied the poems (over-studying the prosody, to my mind) within the scope of his contention that 'poetry was never his whole existence'.

It is significant that as soon as a critic looks sustainedly at the text, the obvious becomes prodigious: the effort to understand or to paint vividly has so far obscured the simple facts that Byron was little given to sustained thought, preferring images that were visual or attitudes catalogued according to the pathetic fallacy. Byron had no philosophy, was no great social wit, and was not even essentially a writer. This is not to debunk Byron but to penetrate the mist of Byronism. He thought best when malicious; his most impressive displays are those in which he grafts a grotesquely inappropriate item on to a revered growth: the crippled outsider devising malign prosthetics to shock the literary bourgeois and their betters.

> *I would to heaven that I were so much clay,*
> *As I am blood, bone, marrow, passion, feeling –*
> *Because at least the past were pass'd away –*
> *And for the future – (but I write this reeling. . . .*

The Hamlet-like mood is convincing, and then it is defiled with gusto:

> *Having got drunk exceedingly to-day,*
> *So that I seem to stand upon the ceiling)*
> *I say – the future is a serious matter –*
> *And so – for God's sake – hock and soda-water!*

Reduce everything he ever wrote, and you will find an essential act of repulsion: either self-emptying into a *persona*, or a repudiation. He pushes away what he is; he repudiates even the *persona* of *Don Juan*. He has the insecure person's fierce need of elimination; he needs to feel unobliged to his subject-matter, his friends, his publisher, his mistresses, his house, his rôle, his reputation. And yet, by a method approaching 'double-think', he seeks to eliminate this lust for elimination; and so he lands up with inappropriate impedimenta – the wrong woman, the wrong type of poem, the wrong reputation, the wrong stanza-form, and so on. His was a multiple nature, chameleonic and irresponsible. This is not to say that he cannot be found in a mood of single-mindedness, a denial of his changeability, a resolute act – all of which show now and then in his dealings over his daughters. Simply, his inconsistency amounted to a perpetual recombination of the same (or most of the same) elements.

There were limits to his unpredictability. He is never to be found propounding a philosophical scheme. He is never the thorough classicist or the thorough romantic. But there is, in the life and in the legend of Byronism, plenty enough; enough, in one person and one life, of other humans and their suppressed cravings to keep the rehashers busy for decades to come. What needs to be undertaken is a study of the literary implications of this much-quarried temperament. The personality, I suggest, pre-empts the style and the genre. Here was a sensitive man who for social and psychic reasons had to eliminate ties and sensibility. Only when he wrote farcically or confessionally was he a writer without reserve. And when he wrote confession-ally he was eventually obliged to evoke *Childe Harold*. Even in *Don Juan* he can be sincerely himself only when writing from the viewpoint of farce. For in farce there is no considerateness, no sensitivity and no response. The personages are inhuman; they lack 'presence' – in its religious sense, and are not *obliged* in any way. And, in Byron's writing, just as there is a farce of personages, there is – consummate in *Don Juan* – a farce of language. The serious poet at his dignified best or portentous worst is obliged to maintain a high seriousness, to ensure congruity and decorum. From all this, the *farceur* is exempt. So

13

it is that Byron develops into the master of hyperbole and bathos, the verbal ostler yoking heterogeneous images by violence together, the arch reducer and inflater, the mutilator crassly misrelating by rhyme, the raper of decorum.

Such a performer could assail with impunity; reputation he had lost but could disregard; ideas he handled laxly – his work testifies that epigrammatists have no monopoly of shallow thinking:

> A row of gentlemen along the streets
> Suspended, may illuminate mankind,
> As also bonfires made of country-seats;
> But the old way is best for the purblind:
> The other looks like phosphorus on sheets,
> A sort of ignis fatuus to the mind,
> Which, though 'tis certain to perplex and frighten,
> Must burn more mildly ere it can enlighten.

He aims at the maximum of maxim with the minimum of sincerity – a fraudulent, self-mocking sage. The pleasure we get from this is that of the combinations: they are unexpected and sudden. The astonishing thing is that the rhyme leads the sententiousness by the nose and yanks it into being. The rest is easy, for euphony and neatness ensure for the content an attention it hardly merits as thought. But this is not deception: to read Don Juan is to engage in a conspiracy against some putative bourgeoisie of the mind – those who think poetry should be sincere, edifying and craftly. Instead, we are to let the gustily confidential manner ('a little quietly facetious upon everything') bounce us into a disorganized hoax. Don Juan is the creation of the bored and sloppy puppeteer, but only in so far as people are concerned. After all, if you think life ridiculous, it matters little what aspect of it you select to prove your point. Into the bargain, Byron's epigraph to the poem indicates, in addition to other things, that there will be no respecting of persons or even of facts: '"Dost thou think, because thou art virtuous, there shall be no more cakes and ale? Yes, by Saint Anne, and ginger shall be hot i' the mouth too!" (*Twelfth Night, or What You Will*).' But the word-play of the poem is brilliant and ingenious – the poet works by denotation alone, thus ensuring a clash now and then of connotations:

> But first of little Leila we'll dispose;
> For like a day-dawn she was young and pure,
> Or like the old comparison of snows,
> Which are more pure than pleasant to be sure.

His policy is clear: any 'old comparison' is to be upset, made to look silly. The aim is not the serious one of minting phrases for posterity to treasure. Rather, it is something more casual and ephemeral; disrespect for the solemnized verbal union and travesty of rhyming decorum:

> Her thoughts were theorems, her words a problem,
> As if she deem'd that mystery would ennoble 'em.

It is the inaccuracy which is funny, with its echo of the slangy impropriety – 'nobble 'em'. In order to secure that effect of stumbling invention and lapsing taste, the poet has to be a satirist, certainly; but more too. He owes no allegiances; and it has always seemed to me that the need to eliminate was fulfilled much more nearly to Byron's satisfaction in his farce with literary language than in his 1816 hegira to the Continent.

Writing, not without a sneer, the *Childe Harold* his public wanted, Byron served up cold the necessary fodder. He was well qualified to do it; and it helped him to become intimate with words without respecting them. (This is not the place for scabrous and perhaps exciting parallels.) Snubbed at Lady Jersey's party on the 8th April 1816, he took off two weeks later and eventually ridiculed the literary etiquette of his despised contemporaries. The more repudiated he was, the more he needed to pass muster, and the more he had to resort to sour grapes. He is one of the most isolated figures in literature; he was lonely early on; and, late, he feared even to cherish the principle of elimination itself – for fear of being typed once again. The ironic disclaimers are ready built-in, in the same way as his need was. His style does not develop, does not improve between *English Bards* (1809) and *Don Juan*. He rejects unsuitable verse-forms as he goes, and singles out the *ottava rima*. But his only advance, other than that from impudent to prudent choice, is from the compact to the sprawling, from the portentous to the knack of making it look preposterous as he winks at the reader and disclaims deep interest in the whole thing anyway.

We do him no injustice, I suggest, if we formulate his compulsions in the following terms. Sensitive, he dissembled as he matured. Wishing to identify loneliness with independence, he turned into farce his legend and his sensitivity. He blunted all his responses, to people, style and ideas. He thus found himself perfectly equipped for literary farce – and yet able to preserve his paradoxical nature by the greatest commitment and response of all, in Greece. In a few words, he is elimination, farce and paradox.

The need to eliminate suggests parallels with Hemingway, who himself sees life as a farce vitiated by sensitivity. The impulse towards farce as an absolute resembles Baudelaire's cult of evil: Byron cares too little, Baudelaire too much; Byron's farce is turbulent and extends to a skilful disrespect for words; Baudelaire's evil is ordered and finicking. Yet both poets are led to the position of unfeeling – Byron by his experiments with words and adamant formula of depreciation, Baudelaire by his cult of the mineral and inanimate. Yet we must be careful here; Byron's disregard for words is a special verbal skill – a superb sense of the incongruous betokening an equal sense of the opposite – while Baudelaire's verse, for all its lapidary polish, presents both *trouvaille* and *cliché*, both the lovingly chiselled and the thoughtlessly taken over.

From an examination and comparison of these two writers with Byron, it is possible to deduce something about the type of literary sophistication the three required – the sophistication of the inanimate; the inability to hope becoming the rage to efface.

There are few of Byron's works which present a subtle and balanced attitude to life; *The Two Foscari* is one of the few. Usually he is out of touch with reality: in *Childe Harold* he either catalogues without responding or sets down feelings which flood the object contemplated. The romances are stereotyped and artificial, rather like first drafts for an Errol Flynn film-script – satisfactory in their kind but lacking convincingness. *The Vision of Judgment* is superb fun. *Beppo* is the idyll travestied by the new standard of irony. And *Don Juan*, urbane and disconcerting to anyone but its author, is a patchwork of distorted sequences and repudiated values, a sustained hoot at social pieties. The other poems are melodramatic and over-simplified:

> *His lip was silent, scarcely beat his heart,*
> *His eye alone proclaim'd, 'We will not part!*
> *Thy band may perish, or thy friends may flee,*
> *Farewell to life, but not adieu to thee!'*

It has taken Hemingway his full writing career to see his way to *The Old Man and the Sea* in which, for the first time, he can see any value in suffering. There is no need to recapitulate his own *via negativa* mitigated only by concocted mystiques of walking on snow or pine-needles, of fondling a well-oiled holster, of simple inarticulate love between doomed sensitives. It is the idyll preserving man from complete apathy – an idyll

longed for with almost childish purity of hope. Byron is a
similar case:

> We wither from our youth, we gasp away –
> Sick – sick; unfound the boon, unslaked the thirst,
> Though to the last, in verge of our decay,
> Some phantom lures, such as we sought at first –
> But all too late, – so are we doubly curst.
>
> Few – none – find what they love or could have loved,
> Though accident, blind contact, and the strong
> Necessity of loving, have removed
> Antipathies. . . .

Hemingway's Big Two-Hearted River and the good fish have
their Byronic counterparts:

> And on thy happy shore a Temple still,
> Of small and delicate proportion, keeps,
> Upon a mild declivity of hill,
> Its memory of thee; beneath it sweeps
> Thy current's calmness; oft from out it leaps
> The finny darter with the glittering scales. . . .

Byron's narrative and reflective poems are packed with images
of purgation and aspiration, yearnings to cleanse and outstrip.
The civilized temperament, he seems to say, cannot bear very
much reality, and must disburden itself by outpourings or by
insulating itself: the Childe or the 'Dumb Ox'. The outbursts
in Hemingway are few, but produce a colossal effect of cloud-
burst; his usual manner is the pregnant laconic with the sensitive reader doing all the work of inference. In this way the
characters are exempted from rhetoric, and Hemingway himself from formulating a despair best left inchoate.

The distinction to be made between the insulations of
Hemingway and Byron is that the former suppresses feeling in
a very obvious way; Byron derides it:

'Tis said that their last parting was pathetic,
As partings often are, or ought to be,
And their presentiment was quite prophetic,
That they should never more each other see,
(A sort of morbid feeling, half poetic,
Which I have known occur in two or three,)
When kneeling on the shore upon her sad knee
He left his Adriatic Ariadne.

Notice the variety of the derisory method. He opens with a slightly bored evocation of hearsay, capping the lack of sympathy with a bathetic alliteration (parting/pathetic) — a conspired accident immediately backed by the blasé sententiousness of 'As partings often are'. Sophistication means being (or seeming to be) familiar with everything. So, in this stanza, the alternatives become blasé remoteness from the trite or equally blasé chiding of the irregular: disdain or mockery. Follows another crass alliteration. The 'pathetic/prophetic' rhyme is already plangent; the context grants it a polysyllabic idiocy worthy of Dickens. The fifth line is doleful lumps. Then, jocularly insentient, 'Which I have known occur . . .' evoking the pomposity that cannot survive the cloudy irony of 'two or three', he makes a quick execution by the awkward route of 'sad knee' – housemaid's, water on it, tears, incongruous posture – and leaves the image to flounder amidst a context of epic although pathetic associations.

At the far end of this scale are those war photographs of the smiling hanged, and at different points along it are the clown's bulbous nose, The Three Stooges, Pantaloon, the midget wrestlers, the hairy woman, distorting mirrors and the grotesque practical jokes of Peter the Great. It is easy to make the human ridiculous, and with varying degrees of savagery. The professional discomfiters and despoilers who boast their devotion to reality are usually envious of what they attack. But nihilism can be equally well the attitude of the wholly disgusted and the wholly hopeless: Dadaism, Hemingway's *nada*, Lear's 'Nothing will come of nothing' and his 'Never, never, never, never, never.' It amounts to the philosophical hysteria of great wits approaching madness. The small *planche de salut* – say, Hemingway's 'Clean Well Lighted Place' or Byron's independence in Italy – is usually sufficient to preserve the thin partition between *saeva indignatio* and madness. We may think of Swift's child-language, Dowson's infatuation with a small girl, Gide's Bach – of something to set our psychic watches by, something like the regular walking of Emmanuel Kant. The fiercer spirits need their anodyne, especially if they have no fulcrum – unfixed in principles and place. Byron kept his balance by strict apathy, by not undergoing; or, to be more accurate, by managing in public a performance which depended on such apathy. Within the rakish nonchalance of *Don Juan* Byron goes through the motions of alienating himself from the usual human condition. Live! he will let his servants do that for him:

> *Revenge in person's certainly no virtue,*
> *But then 'tis not my fault, if others hurt you.*

And when he seems to care, to be for once enthusiastic and responsive, he is tantalizing or really up to something else:

> *Her eye (I'm very fond of handsome eyes)*
> *Was large and dark. . . .*

That ostentatiously casual unbending apes the prodigies of confession: usually in this poem, Byron intends only to jeer and depreciate, to parade a witty *insouciance* or a crippling self-consciousness:

> *. . . charms in her as natural*
> *As sweetness to the flower, or salt to ocean,*
> *Her zone to Venus, or his bow to Cupid*
> *(But this last simile is trite and stupid).*

He shows himself only in order to be pointless or to vitiate. He uses the couplet in the *ottava rima* much in the manner of a ringmaster. He calls us to order:

> *She sits upon his knee, and drinks his sighs,*
> *He hers, until they end in broken gasps;*
> *And thus they form a group that's quite antique,*
> *Half naked, loving, natural and Greek.*

The type of sincere, spontaneous and primitive compassion that the characters in Hemingway's short story *The Killers* dare not express, because they fear to become involved, is the type that Byron mocks. Hemingway suppresses to commend; Byron expresses to disdain.

And it is here that Byron seems near to Baudelaire. Here is M. Escarpit's version of the self-conscious Byron: the poet, his own *voyeur*, 'observes to find matter for meditation, meditates the better to observe, and, one may add, the better to observe himself meditating and observing'. This is the perfect Chinese box of Narcissism; and Baudelaire was very similar. He too could never forget himself. The sexual act entailed remaining a solitary, an onanist. One wore spiritual gloves at it. One went outside oneself and studied the act from the ceiling. Oneself – that was a thing, like other things; and other things were mere pretexts for self-scrutiny. This possessive solitude he shares with Byron. Both found themselves rejected; both chose solitude purposely so that it should not be inflicted by others. Both felt unique. Both, though appearing to live, lov and participate, refused themselves to others. Their pride fed on itself. Their sensibility rejected the natural in all its forms, eschewed immediacy. Their problem was to intensify awareness of themselves without the contrast of others. Compare

> *Tête-à-tête sombre et limpide*
> *Qu'un cœur devenu son miroir!*

and

Je suis la plaie et le couteau
Et la victime et le bourreau.

with

All suffering doth destroy, or is destroy'd,
Even by the sufferer. . . .

and

I live not in myself, but I become
Portion of that around me. . . .

Is it not better, then, to be alone,
And love Earth only for its earthly sake?

.   .   .   .   .   .

Is it not better thus our lives to wear,
Than join the crushing crowd, doom'd to inflict or bear?

But for both of them it was bound to fail. Baudelaire allowed himself to drift, Childe-like: '. . . what I feel is an immense discouragement, a sense of unbearable isolation. . . .' But he had to have someone to offend: 'When I've inspired universal horror and disgust, I shall have overcome solitude.' Compare this with Byron's 'What I feel most growing upon me are laziness, and a disrelish more powerful than indifference.' He wished 'to lose (his) own wretched identity': that is, he wanted to shed what others had made him, and to remake himself according to his own whim. In Venice, as a pariah gossiped about by palazzo and gondolier alike, he possessed a social function: his oddity was nigh-institutional. He lived up to the legend of his Childe, and went further into a contemptuous uniqueness of the *bête de luxe*. As he went on, he seemed to live only for oblivions; he lapsed, drifted, confounded every confusion and yet remained capable of the final though grudging *ascêsis* and that boisterous long poem, *Don Juan*.

Why? We can only guess. He was acutely self-conscious but lacked self-knowledge. Pessimistic too, he was never thoroughly

bitter. He was incapable of an absolute attitude, and his sense
of the ridiculous never died. Perhaps, after leaving his half-
sister, Mrs Leigh, he never really became involved again.
Perhaps he used her, once he realized that she would remain
unattainable, as an excuse for a deep self-sufficiency undisturbed
by whatever turmoil his life became. She came to symbolize
his own state of unavailability: 'that perfect and boundless
attachment which bounds and binds me to you'; '*mine* for you
is the union of all passions and of all affections . . .'; 'whenever
I love anything it is because it reminds me of you'. The time
came when he no longer had to be 'present' to her, or to others,
because he could delude himself that his best was invested in her.

It is tempting to compare with the following:

During my childhood there was a period when I loved you passion-
ately. . . . I was always living in you; you belonged to me alone.
You were at once an idol and a friend.

That is Baudelaire writing to his mother, Mme Aupick, the
only person he ever loved; the person whose letters were manna
and had often to be carried in his pocket for days until he was
in a suitable frame of mind. She was, like Augusta Leigh,
capricious, gullible and an opportunist. She was the Mother-
Confessor in whose eyes Baudelaire had to redeem himself.
She was the obverse of his *nostalgie de la boue*. About Augusta
Leigh, too, there was something of the intimate idol. But the
methods of self-defilement that Byron and Baudelaire adopted
were quite different. Both had a spiritual prop that was nearly
incestuous; but Baudelaire pursued an absolute of evil, Byron
of immunity. Baudelaire's pursuit was disciplined and scrupulous, Byron's chaotic and careless. Baudelaire, yearning for an
absolute attitude, invented an absolute life. Byron's sense of
humour destroyed his poses; Baudelaire never did anything as
natural as to guffaw. Byron's only universal attitude was con-
tempt; Baudelaire had to take things seriously, and Byron could

never do that for long. For excess, incest, pederasty, dandyism, narcissism, and for shaping in exile insentient personalities, they go together. Each aimed at making himself invulnerable, and each sought to keep the treasured image (Mme Aupick, Mrs Leigh) undefiled by debauchery. Both had their share of bravado. But Baudelaire banned the natural, pored over and revised his manuscripts, worshipped order. Byron just submitted; yielded to the natural, ignored order and even affected an ostentatious carelessness. Baudelaire's *dandyisme* was a religion, Byron's a fad and an indulgence. To Baudelaire the poet was a priest, to Byron a mere practitioner.

The fact is that Byron was over-endowed where Baudelaire had too little. Byron's poetry was lava, not mosaic. He was a man of the world; Baudelaire made his own world. Byron's vice was that of the sophisticate: over-familiarity with everything. Baudelaire's was to see everything as a child might. Byron submitted; Baudelaire refused. So Byron could disdain where Baudelaire abolished.

Beyond this point the comparison becomes unprofitable. We can see already how Byron was not self-conscious enough as an artist to need the absolute of Baudelaire, and how Baudelaire resented the gratuitous in art. Baudelaire's art was his social class; Byron, never quite *déclassé*, needed art less, lived in his art less, and so found himself easier to escape – 'to lose my own wretched identity'. He could escape into writing; but Baudelaire, too familiar with himself, could hardly recognize himself in the abstract or in the glass. That is why he falsified his appearance, in order to make *something* visible.

The one thing Byron could isolate and protect was himself: this was the advantage of moving in society and of being enmeshed. Baudelaire never quite knew where he himself ended and others began; and so his protective gestures abolished where Byron's fended off.

This distinction emerges more vividly if we look at the

second version of *l'Ivrogne* – a play Baudelaire sketched out
but never completed. The husband tries to make love to his
wife in a deserted spot. She refuses him. Half-suspicious, he
sends her down a lane at the end of which there is a well. In
the darkness, 'if she escapes so much the better. If she falls in,
it's God who condemns her.' Such witchcraft enables us to
shelve responsibility: Baudelaire isn't going to meddle. As far
as he is concerned, the problem has to be abolished. It must not
be solved by rape or murder. Compare this with Byron's
outburst after hearing that Sir Samuel Romilly had committed
suicide. (Romilly had taken a retaining fee from Byron and had
later acted in Lady Byron's interest.)

Sir Samuel Romilly has cut his throat for the loss of his wife. It is
now nearly three years since he became, in the face of his compact . . .
the advocate of the measures and the Approver of the proceedings,
which deprived me of mine . . . . It was not in vain that I invoked
Nemesis in the midnight of Rome from the awfullest of her
ruins. . . .

What is he doing here? Certainly he is trying his rhetoric,
playing at an infallible witchcraft after the event. Is there too,
amid the bragging pose, a serious assertion that by their own
actions his harmers condemn themselves? To lay too much
emphasis on this squib would be unwise; but it is possible to see
a parody here of his disaffection extending into magical
invulnerability. He does not have to meddle, even to exact
revenge. But where Baudelaire's protagonist left well alone
when he could have acted directly, Byron's chance of action
was as remote as his fancy was avid. To believe, even in jest,
that such invocations work, you have to have agile imagination
as well as an enfeebled sense of human intercourse. Byron, of
course, didn't take it seriously; but he had only a single-minded
response to the suicide – he responded only in so far as his
loathing prompted. There is paranoia here, and spleen. Neither
is in keeping with the gentlemanly rebukes to Polidori, his

personal travelling physician; but Byron did not have to be in his maddest phase in order to toy with fantasies like these. They accorded with his grandiose idea of his own uniqueness, and they suited admirably the requirements of his *Don Juan* period.

In fact, he had lived much of his life in the spirit in which he wrote *Don Juan*: disaffected, escapist yet always mercurial enough to travesty the parboiled attitude. With, as Peter Quennell puts it, his emotional capital squandered, he continued to enjoy watching and staging the gambles of others. These subjects were still worth turning a verse upon – turning with a veneer of toughness and knowledgeable importunity:

> *She thought to stab herself, but then she had*
> *The dagger close at hand, which made it awkward;*
> *For Eastern stays are little made to pad,*
> *So that a poniard pierces if 'tis stuck hard:*
> *She thought of killing Juan – but, poor lad!*
> *Though he deserved it well for being so backward,*
> *The cutting off his head was not the art*
> *Most likely to attain her aim – his heart.*

We must not confuse the exposure of foible with bitter feeling on the author's part. Indeed, to attempt such exposure is to hold nihilism at bay; and Byron's position in *Don Juan* is far subtler than despair. Unable to attain and exploit an absolute – of evil, purity, romance, melancholy – he found in farce, characteral and verbal, a form in which no aspect of the poem's heterogeneousness had to blend artistically with any other. He could get away with a mixture; he would 'melo' the drama.

All his life, apart from such episodes as his 1812 speech in the Lords against the death penalty for the Nottingham Frame-Breakers and his resolve to learn Armenian, he had been unable to integrate his personality in terms of a realizable ideal. Similarly, he had been unable to express his personality in full. He lacked roots, both social and literary. But in *Don Juan* he shovelled together in cavalier fashion all the elements within him. The gauche and stagey he castigated; he released with benign severity a matured disillusion; he exploited to the full his gift for incongruity; he even brought off some moving lyrical passages; but, most of all, he gave the poem the authentic rhythm of life, its suffocating detail and full extent. There is no philosophy, but plenty of philosophizing. The imagery of the poem is staggeringly original and wide-ranging. The stanza was just right, with the final couplet ever-ready to sabotage the preceding six lines. But this is not the place for an analysis of the style. What is important is to remember that the poem is mature work; that the disillusion is not uncynical; that even if Byron is not making his own deepest feelings available, he lets his characters behave naturally. He himself appears only in his rôle of the slapdash impresario:

> *I don't much like describing people mad,*
> *For fear of seeming rather touch'd myself –*

And his main pleasure seems to be in the exquisite misalliance that was his farce with the literary language. His gesture of defiance was to conflict with an established order of conduct and style; he needed to conflict, and he put up a pretty convincing vindication of his methods. Here are two excerpts from his mordant Preface to Cantos VI-VIII (1823) of *Don Juan*:

With regard to the objections which have been made on another score to the already published cantos of this poem, I shall content myself with two quotations from Voltaire: 'La pudeur s'est enfuite des coeurs, et s'est réfugiée sur les lèvres'. 'Plus les moeurs sont dépravés, plus les expressions deviennent mesurées; on croit regagner en language ce qu'on a perdu en vertu.'

This is the real fact, as applicable to the degraded and hypocritical mass which leavens the present English generation, and is the only answer they deserve. . . . *cant.* . . . is the crying sin of this double-dealing and false-speaking time of selfish spoilers, and – but enough for the present.

He has not altered a great deal since the 'caustic' offered in *English Bards and Scotch Reviewers*. He may spice with gibes, but he has clear standards in mind. The animus is more than personal. And *Don Juan*, as Gifford said, was 'the only sincere thing' he had written. We might add, the poem in which he was sincere about the most, the poem in which nothing succeeded like restless excess, in spite of the 'negative and polemical working' that Matthew Arnold deplored.

Chapter 2

VERSE IN ITS PLACE

What has put Byron out of favour with the public of late, is
not his faults, but his excellences. His artistic good taste, his
classical polish, his sound shrewd sense, his hatred of cant, his
insight into humbug, above all, his shallow, pitiable habit of
being always intelligible: these are the sins. . . .

(CHARLES KINGSLEY)

BYRON'S attitude to his art was far from messianic. Not for
him the fee-fi-fo-fum of the sublime seer, the pallor of the
spiritual communicant, the intense effort towards negative
capability. He wrote to entertain his age and, it is worth remark-
ing, himself. Poetry was the 'lava of the imagination', 'the
dream of [his] sleeping passions', the emblem of a personality.
It was an extension of diurnal excitement, calling of course for
labour and wit, but never more than the manipulable by-product
of a seething spirit. Byron formed these views early and never
rejected them. In the Preface to the first edition of *Hours of
Idleness* (1807), he attempted to disarm the critics with an
ingenuous-looking admission:

Some few were written during the disadvantages of illness and
depression of spirits: under the former influence, 'Childish Recol-
lections', in particular, were composed. This consideration, though
it cannot excite the voice of praise, may at least arrest the arm of
censure.

Why? Because, he seems to assume, none of this is very important, and no one minds stretching a point in order to indulge a
guileless tiro! After all, it isn't a public affair, and 'Poetry . . . is
not my primary vocation; to divert the dull moments of indis-
position, or the monotony of a vacant hour, urged me "to
this sin": little can be expected from so unpromising a muse'.

But the little sin was blasted by the critics, and the young sinner soon changed his tone. He gained a good deal in sophistication too: he had asserted that 'To produce anything entirely new, in an age so fertile in rhyme, would be a Herculean task, as every subject has already been treated to its utmost extent . . . and I shall never attempt to . . . pluck a single additional sprig from groves where I am, at best, an intruder'. He had resigned himself to becoming one of 'the mob of gentlemen who write'. No doubt this preface was shot through with sincerity; it was also spiced with a taste of the polysyllabic gibes that were to follow in *Don Juan*:

. . . 'The Catalogue of Royal and Noble Authors', – a work to which the Peerage is under infinite obligations, inasmuch as many names of considerable length, sound, and antiquity, are thereby rescued from the obscurity which unluckily overshadows several voluminous productions of their illustrious bearers.

Once he had survived the firing squad of *The Edinburgh Review* and refused to be 'turned from the career of (his) humour by quibbles quick, and paper bullets of the brain', his writing career rapidly took shape. He became a close scrutineer of his contemporaries, an implacable literary saboteur and a prolific experimenter. *Childe Harold* appeared in February 1812, and ran through seven editions in five weeks. Byron was made – and unmade. But whether, in the subsequent years, he lived or resisted a life *en caractère,* grappled with lameness, money troubles, open and secret liaisons, a dawdling publisher and the long backwash of scandal, he kept after the reviewers. More important, however, he seriously tried to evolve the type of poetic entertainment that suited both his talents and his age.

He was a serious inquirer into poetics – not a Keats, but a student of entertainment. His tastes and prejudices were always clear: his life in one aspect was the prolonged excoriation of

Robert Southey – in Byron's eye, the arch dunce and literary felon of the age. In his *Journal* of 1813 Byron drew up 'a triangular *Gradus ad Parnassum*' and at the peak placed Sir Walter Scott – 'undoubtedly the Monarch of Parnassus, and the most *English* of bards'. Next – 'the last of the *best* school' – he put Rogers; below him, Moore and Campbell. Below these two come Southey, Wordsworth and Coleridge; and, below them, 'the Many'. 'I have ranked the names upon my triangle more upon what I believe popular opinion, than any decided opinion of my own'—his afterthought perhaps explains his omission of Crabbe and Mrs Felicia Dorothea Hemans; and in 1813 Shelley's best was unwritten. But was Byron really capable of judging? He looked back to Dryden, Pope and Rochester. In the *Notes* to *Don Juan* there appears in damning isolation this excerpt from Wordsworth's *Preface* to the second edition of *Lyrical Ballads* (1800): 'The verses of Dryden, once highly celebrated, are forgotten.' Elsewhere in these *Notes* Wordsworth is more comprehensively and articulately anathematized. (Byron had praised the early Wordsworth but could not stand his later incarnation as 'arch-apostle of mystery and mysticism' and social conformist.)

Wordsworth's place may be in the Customs – it is, I think, in that or the Excise – besides another at Lord Lonsdale's table, where this poetical charlatan and political parasite licks up the crumbs with a hardened alacrity; the converted Jacobin having long subsided into the clownish sycophant of the worst prejudices of the aristocracy.

This is compelling, to say the least; a little *voulu* perhaps and over-adjectival, it drowns rather than demolishes. But Byron was self-critical too: 'I am convinced,' he wrote to John Murray, 'the more I think of it that . . . *all* of us – Scott, Southey, Wordsworth, Moore, Campbell, I – are in the wrong, one as much as another; that we are upon a wrong revolutionary poetical system, or systems, not worth a damn in itself, and

from which none but Rogers and Crabbe are free; and that the
present and next generations will finally be of this opinion. I
am the more confirmed in this by having lately gone over some
of our classics, particularly Pope. . . . I took Moore's poems and
my own and some others, and went over them side by side
with Pope's, and I was really astonished . . . and mortified at
the ineffable distance in point of sense, harmony, effect, and
even *Imagination*, passion, and *Invention*, between the little
Queen Anne's man, and us of the Lower Empire. Depend upon
it, it is all Horace then, and Claudian now . . . and if I had to
begin again, I would model myself accordingly.' In *Hints from
Horace* he predicts that 'those shall sink, which now appear to
thrive', and gives Horatian reasons:

> *The greater portion of the rhyming tribe*
> *(Give ear, my friend, for thou hast been a scribe)*
> *Are led astray by some peculiar lure.*
> *I labour to be brief – become obscure;*
> *One falls while following elegance too fast;*
> *Another soars, inflated with bombast;*
> *Too low a third crawls on, afraid to fly,*
> *He spins his subject to satiety;*
> *Absurdly varying, he at last engraves*
> *Fish in the woods, and boars beneath the waves!*

All of this is sententious enough. But he constructs an aesthetic
of his own as well:

> *The slow, sad stanza will correctly paint*
> *The lover's anguish, or the friend's complaint.*

Blank verse, he complains, rarely quits tragedy's side; comedy
has descended to prose. Rhyme no longer appeals to dramatists.
He takes the routine swipe at Southey ('whose epic mountains
never fail in mice'), another at Bowles (with whom he dis-
puted in 1821 about Pope) and then another at Johnson's

Irene ('We saved Irene but half-damn'd the play'). He bemoans the general low state of the drama 'fettered by whig Walpole': 'Men go not to be lectured but amused.' There is too much prescription, he says; sensibility is too rigid, taste has become a cultivated commodity:

> *The dirty language, and the noisome jest,*
> *Which pleased in Swift of yore, we now detest.* . . .

It is the age of criticism, false gentility and humourlessness. Pomposity and pedantry rule together:

> *With little rhyme, less reason, if you please,*
> *The name of poet may be got with ease.* . . .

Only Rogers and Crabbe, to whom he adds the Sheffield poet Montgomery, remain uncontaminated. What really puzzled Byron was the lack of an accepted poetic manner. Where Wordsworth sought to widen, others tried to constrict. Demotic idiom caused a flutter among the literati and a defensive narrowing in bourgeois taste – both as regards idiom and subject.

Byron, of course, was a realist and a jester: he was lucky enough to get away with (to borrow his phrase) Gothic daring in English money. Indecisive as his poetic practice was, his farcical gifts showed early and kept on showing – although not always in his poetry. It is in the prefaces, postscripts and notes that the uncertain feline shows his real claws. Indeed, his own judgment of Pope, Dryden and Swift fits himself: '. . ."Mac Flecknoe", the "Dunciad", and all Swift's lampooning ballads. Whatever their other works may be, these originated in personal feelings, and angry retort on unworthy rivals; and though the ability of these satires elevates the poetical, their poignancy detracts from the personal character of the writer(s).' Possibly; but this is no place for appraisals of exemplary conduct. Byron's vituperation often went beyond the object; he enjoyed

c   33

the thing for its own sake. He was nothing if not high-spirited and egregious, and his best performances are in hyperbole and reduction:

> In General Rostopchin's consummate conflagration, the consumption of tallow and train oil was so great, that the market was inadequate to the demand: and thus one hundred and thirty-three thousand persons were starved to death, by being reduced to wholesome diet! The lamplighters of London have since subscribed a pint (of oil) apiece, and the tallow-chandlers have unanimously voted a quantity of best moulds (four to the pound), to the relief of the surviving Scythians. . . .

He has to see people as things, he has to adjust the curiosity to the point of the grotesque. He distorts and damages, First they become inanimate wax; then he melts them slightly and irrevocably. Wherever he plies his skill, the human aspect of the subject is infringed. His vocabulary fathers the vituperation, the words become objects in themselves, and their author a variety of Mr Punch – the minatory marionette between sadism and paranoia:

> There are also some men with hearts so thoroughly bad, as to remind us of those phenomena often mentioned in natural history; viz. a mass of solid stone – only to be opened by force – and when divided you discover a toad in the centre, lively, and with the reputation of being venomous.

> I suppose next year he will be entitled the 'Virgin Mary': if so, Lord George Gordon himself would have nothing to object to such liberal bastards of our Lady of Babylon.

> I thought Fitzgerald had been the tail of poesy; but, alas, he is only the penultimate.

But on occasion, he neither colours nor organizes; he calls Southey 'that poor insane creature', Stott 'the most impudent and execrable of literary poachers'. He alludes grimly to 'the poor idiots of the Lakes', Landor's 'trash' and the 'dirty pack' of *The Edinburgh Review*. Straight abuse, however, detains him little. His attacks, polarized between 'soaring Southey' and 'grovelling Stott', are creative. The words intoxicate him – 'the gross flattery, the dull impudence, the renegado intolerance, and impious cant' – and where hatred cannot goad him, he is tempted by the love of fun. He mocks through a mask of cumbrous pomp:

I omit noticing some edifying Ithyphallics of Savagius, wishing to keep the proper veil over them, if his grave but somewhat indiscreet worshipper will suffer it. . . .

It is possible that some readers may object, in these objectionable times, to the freedom with which saints, angels, and spiritual persons discourse in this 'Vision'. But, for precedents upon such points, I must refer him to Fielding's 'Journey from this World to the next', and to the Visions of myself, the said Quevedo, in Spanish or translated.

It is the elaborate mockery of a complex man whose incredibly fertile invention needed neither target nor direction. It is the intellectual high spirits of *Don Juan* which announce themselves in his prefaces. Above all, it is the boisterousness of the socially awkward person: he has to travesty the tight-ropes he cannot negotiate, execrate the taboos he overlooks and, in the last resort, expel his flippancy without risk of retort.

In the world of words, all this is possible – provided that when you tamper with the lares and penates and the nostrums you cover your tracks. This explains the tergiversations in *Don Juan*: the sudden confidences by the poet, the constantly renewed air of insincerity, the regular disclaimers, the tantalizing way in which the style appears to repudiate the idea, the couplet the sestet, the panache the cynicism. The poem is a whirligig, but it spins unpivoted; and Byron's only sincerity seems to be towards emotions he has lost and tries to recapture:

> *In youth I wrote because my mind was full,*
> *And now because I feel it growing dull.*

The paradise of pleasure and *ennui* has taken its place among the objects, among the bizarre set of props that included Robert Southey, Jeffrey, the petty scribblers, the waltz, Capel Lofft the Cobbler, the voluminous gentry whose rabies was rhyming, the quacks and reformers, the tallow-chandlers, and the ladies in pursuit. This is the mythology of his invective, the ephemeral detritus of literary by-play. In a sense, the by-play was Byron's eighteenth-century self longing for the feuding, lampooning and scurrile scoffing of that century – and, furthermore, needing a worthy opponent. Byron eventually turned his irritability upon the language and, with all the force of rhyme, secured some monstrous couplings. But it was in his vituperative prose writings that he exercised most freely his surrealistic talents – as far back as 'Horace Hornem', who wrote thus 'To The Publisher of *The Waltz*'. His 'letter' is printed at the beginning of the poem:

But, judge of my surprise, on arriving, to see poor dear Mrs Hornem with her arms half round the loins of a huge hussar-looking gentleman I never set eyes on before; and his, to say truth, rather more than half round her waist, turning round and round to a d—d see-saw up-and-down sort of tune, that reminded me of the 'Black Joke', only more '*affettuoso*', till it made me quite giddy with wondering they were not so. By-and-by they stopped a bit, and I thought they would sit or fall down:— but no; with Mrs H.'s hand on his shoulder, '*quam familiariter*', (as Terence said, when I was at school,) they walked about a minute, and then at it again, like two cockchafers spitted on the same bodkin. . . .

He's showing off, but he's also building them up before shrinking them in the last few words. In this he is with Jonson, Dryden and Pope. There is the same rodomontade show of learning, the same impudent parody, wilful frankness and gusto. Joyce's *Ulysses* is within guffawing distance, and there is even a foretaste of Alfred Jarry's poignantly gross joke-play *Ubu Roi*. 'The mind sits terrified', said Sterne, another master of comic hyperbole, 'at the objects she has magnified herself, and blackened; reduce them to their proper size and hue, she overlooks them.'

Byron needed these excesses: fearful of derision he derided first. He flourished in tensions between rhyme's clinching effect and prose's talking quality, between Augustan aesthetic and his imperious instincts, between sensitivity and the fear of being wounded, between generosity and the need to go uncluttered, between romance and farce, living and writing. When he produced his great comic novel in verse, he had yielded to impulse. A born improviser well-endowed with cheek, he wrote in the old lackadaisical way – the way pointed by this note to *The Corsair*:

The opening lines, as far as section ii, have, perhaps, little business here, and were annexed to an unpublished (though printed) poem ['The Curse of Minerva']; but they were written on the spot, in the Spring of 1814, and – I scarce know why – the reader must excuse their appearance here – if he can.

He is as far from an apocalyptic as from an Augustan discipline. He is obliged to affect the manner of picaresque fiction. He is too near the *grand guignol* (however ironic his adjacence) to set himself a standard of decorum: the rude posterior or the knowing eye pops out constantly – just, as it were, to see if we're noticing. Poetry, always a precarious mode of elevation, prescribes conditions of stability; so Byron, diversifying his texture, destroys the illusion. His personality, in other words, exceeded his aesthetic resolve.

Yet he was fully capable of amassing effects flawlessly in verse or prose. The following is a note to *Hints from Horace*:

Mr Southey has lately tied another canister to his tail in the 'Curse of Kehama', maugre the neglect of Madoc etc., and has in one instance had a wonderful effect. A literary friend of mine, walking out one lovely evening last summer, on the eleventh bridge of the

Paddington canal, was alarmed by the cry of 'one in jeopardy':
he rushed along, collected a body of Irish haymakers (supping on
buttermilk in an adjacent paddock), procured three rakes, one eel-
spear, and a landing-net, and at last (horresco referens) pulled out –
his own publisher. The unfortunate man was gone for ever, and so
was a large quarto wherewith he had taken the leap, which proved,
on inquiry, to have been Mr Southey's last work. Its 'alacrity of
sinking' was so great, that it has never since been heard of; though
some maintain that it is at this moment concealed at Alderman
Birch's pastry premises, Cornhill. Be this as it may, the coroner's
inquest brought in a verdict of 'Felo de bibliophilâ' against a
'quarto unknown'; and circumstantial evidence being since strong
against the 'Curse of Kehama' (of which the above words are an
exact description), it will be tried by its peers next session, in Grub
street – Arthur, Alfred, Davideis, Richard Coeur de Lion, Exodus
Exodia, Epigoniad, Calvary, Fall of Cambria, Siege of Acre, Don
Roderick, and Tom Thumb the Great, are the names of the twelve
jurors.

This is genially donnish and yet belongs to that macabre pattern
which takes as its motif the sinner sewn into a sack and dropped
into the Bosphorus. Byron was fascinated by this idea. A note
to *The Giaour* tells us that 'the wife of Muchtar Pacha complained to his father of his son's supposed infidelity; he asked
with whom, and she had the barbarity to give in a list of the
twelve handsomest women in Yanina. They were seized,
fastened up in sacks, and drowned in the lake the same night!
One of the guards who was present informed me', says Byron,
'that not one of the victims uttered a cry, or showed a symptom
of terror, at so sudden a "wrench from all we know, from all
we love".' Byron told the Shelleys he had had the same done
to an unfaithful concubine when he was living in Constanti-
nople. (He was there for just over two months; it sounds, as
Shelley affirmed, like exhibitionism.)

But why did the theme appeal? It satisfied an exotic necro-
phily, true; perhaps the gross packeting and the completeness
of the disposal tugged at the fancy of the inveterate escaper. An

encumbrance could be wrapped up and disposed of; the human could be treated as an object. It is an idea that affiliates itself with Marlowe's suave monster, poisoning wells at night, or with that monumental sequence in *The Jew of Malta*: 'Thou hast committed Fornication: but that was in another country, And besides, the wench is dead.' Or compare with Alfred Jarry's Ubu, armed with his dunghook, his baton of physical apparatus, his *sabre à merdre* and his little bit of wood for poking in ears and noses. 'Oh, no surely,' Ubu says at war, 'it can't be more Russians, I've had enough – and yet after all it's quite simple, if they catch me I will sew them all up.' He is the monstrous incubus – governmental or bestial – who kills the sensitive individual in us, who tampers with and nullifies our allegiances, who gives us a number and a cell. Odd that Byron, the supreme individualist, should have sensed this ogre's value. After all, if you could treat people like pigs, there would be no problems in life. But the problems make it worth while.

The composer of farce, in action or language, toys with a nullity of the sort that Byron must have experienced in the last days when he could not communicate, respond, feel; or explain the sudden withdrawal into self which is perhaps inevitable for any creative person. Beethoven, composing his late *Quartets*, appeared to undergo a similar experience; and we can find parallels by the score: Yeats in his *Autobiographies;* Gide in *The Fruits of the Earth*; Ernst Jünger, the German soldier-writer, in his cult of the nihilistic automaton; Mr Eliot's crustacean longing – 'scuttling across the floors of silent seas'. It has in it more of Garbo than Thoreau or Rousseau: at one extreme the mental cell of the mystic, at the other the ordinary desire to get away from it all – but not to anywhere. *Taedium vitae* prompts a person to be – literally – apathetic: he avoids civilized concourse; he wants to take up no attitude, incur no responsibility. And Byron's early pugnacity hardened into a convenient literary manner – an empty combativeness of someone apparently quite heartless. Once he had found the verse form that suited his miscellaneous self he was able to concentrate on the deployment of images and the peculiar indifference of *Don Juan*, in which people, ideas, objects, sensations, states of mind are treated alike, are regarded on the same level and as of the same kind.

But before he could attempt *Don Juan*, he had to stock up with imagery, perfect his knack of zany conjunctions, and, most of all, clarify his own aesthetic especially with regard to verse forms. Like St Francis, being 'inflamed with a wonderful fervour of the mind, he plunged his naked body into a great heap of snow'. From this anecdote of Butler's, appended to *Don Juan*, Byron evolved his image, a significant one surely, of the 'concubine of snow'. Frigidity, unyielding reception, the inanimate placing the burden of response (or self-delusion) on the instigator – these ideas had their part in Byron's appreciation of form as vessel, not matrix, as something fixed where all is moving, as a container for the living and a packet for the Bosphorus.

He was singularly clear-headed about less private matters, though, and he never minced matters in his prefaces. 'I am aware', he proclaims with the pontifical weariness of twenty-eight years, 'that in modern times the delicacy or fastidiousness of the reader may deem such subjects unfit for the purposes of poetry.' He contemptuously specifies:

The Greek dramatists, and some of the best of our old English writers, were of a different opinion: as Alfieri and Schiller have also been, more recently, upon the Continent.

He even pointed out that a prudish age falsified its facts, especially when love was in question. Adding to the Preface to *Childe Harold* he put his readers straight:

Amongst the many objections made to the very indifferent character of the 'vagrant Childe' (whom, notwithstanding many hints to the contrary, I still maintain to be a fictitious personage), it has been stated, that, besides the anachronism, he is very *unknightly*, as the times of the Knights were times of Love, Honour, and so forth. Now, it so happens that the good old times, when 'l'amour du bon vieux tems, l'amour antique', flourished, were the most profligate of all possible centuries. Those who have any doubts on this subject may consult Sainte-Palaye, *passim*, and more particularly vol. ii. p. 69. The vows of chivalry were no better kept than any other vows whatsoever; and the songs of the Troubadours were not more decent, and certainly were much less refined, than those of Ovid.

A sharp stare at the audience, the pen spiked back into the inkpot, and it is over. Warm with scholarly triumph, he at once resumes the propitiation of his unscholarly following: *Childe Harold* 'never was intended as an example, further than to show, that early perversion of mind and morals leads to satiety of past pleasures and disappointment in new ones. . . . Had I proceeded with the poem, this character would have deepened as he drew to the close; for the outline which I once meant to fill up for him was, with some exceptions, the sketch of a modern Timon.' His transitions are superb: he makes a very thorough job of that special public performance in which the careful scholar attends the impetuous poet. He had a good store of information, and he was proud of it. His prose appendices would yield a quaint anthology: there is spleen and vituperation in plenty; but there are all sorts of tit-bits of information gracefully imparted. There are student rambles at Cambridge; notes on Shakespeare, Menander and Sappho; asides on *Ossian*, Turkish customs, Locke and Captain Bligh; discourses on Albanian folk-songs, factual errors in Bacon, Venetian society and manners, as well as jottings on angling, Marathon ('The plain of Marathon was offered to me for sale at the sum of sixteen thousand piastres, about nine hundred pounds') and Lucullus – 'A cherry-tree may weigh against a bloody laurel').

A man so various, one is tempted to say, didn't really need to write poetry. And his poetry is as various as he is: it is, as everyone says, journalistic; sweet or sour confectionery. But the sheer variety of his imagery has been little commented on. Especially in the satirical works, there is a kaleidoscopic quality rare in the poetry of his century. Reading *Don Juan* rather quickly is like viewing the paintings of Chagall in quick succession – the objects soar out at us; gravity, the sullen landlord, is dispossessed; and the merest pretext holds them together:

> *Babel was Nimrod's hunting-box, and then*
> *A town of gardens, walls, and wealth amazing,*
> *Where Nebuchadonosor, king of men,*
> *Reign'd, till one summer's day he took to grazing,*
> *And Daniel tamed the lions in their den,*
> *The people's awe and admiration raising:*
> *'Twas famous, too, for Thisbe and for Pyramus,*
> *And the calumniated queen Semiramis.*

There is no irrelevance here. If the amount of imagery used seems out of proportion to what is said, a compulsive vocabulary and an effervescent mind are to blame – if there need be blame. For this is the collection on show, after the long years of compilation. We are supposed to watch the pranks in texture and structure, not to assess congruities.

But before he became a law unto himself, Byron concerned himself a good deal with congruity and likeness to life. He censured 'The Lay of the Last Minstrel' for having a plan both 'incongruous and absurd': 'the biography of Gilpin Horner, and the marvellous pedestrian page, who travelled twice as fast as his master's horse, without the aid of seven-league boots, are *chefs-d'œuvre* in the improvement of taste'. He is asking for convincingness, but he by no means intends to reduce his request to absurdity; where likeness to life is not attempted, other criteria apply. So, the entire action of *The Vision of Judgment* takes place, as he blandly points out, outside heaven. 'The reader is also requested to observe, that no doctrinal tenets are insisted upon or discussed; that the person of the Deity is carefully withheld from sight. . . . Chaucer's 'Wife of Bath', Pulci's 'Morgante Maggiore', Swift's 'Tale of a Tub', . . . are cases in point of the freedom with which saints etc. may be permitted to converse in works not intended to be serious.' As always, amid the crackle of facetiousness, there is a serious point seriously made. There are no laws for fantasy, he says; you have to invent your own. The preface to *Cain* explains this further:

The author has by no means taken the same liberties with his subject which were common formerly. . . . The author has endeavoured to preserve the language adapted to his characters; and where it is (and this is but rarely) taken from the actual *Scripture*, he has made as little alteration, even of words, as the rhythm would permit. . . . With regard to the language of Lucifer, it was difficult for me to make him talk like a clergyman upon the same subjects; but I have done what I could to restrain him within the bounds of spiritual politeness.

But, later, he had the sense to realize that *Don Juan* could be as artificial as the comedy of humours. In fact, although he extolled the disciplined texture of Pope and Dryden, he saw that their aesthetic of structure was lax. *Lamia, Hyperion, Prometheus Unbound* and *The Triumph of Life* are more carefully conceived than the *Essay on Man, The Dunciad, Absalom and Achitophel* and *MacFlecknoe*. Byron liked to spread himself without too much forethought. Of *Childe Harold* he said, 'A fictitious character is introduced for the sake of giving some connexion to the piece; which, however, makes no pretensions to regularity.' The Childe, 'a very repulsive personage' according to Byron, was really the transplanted sensitive plant, exhaling an odour of well-bred brooding.

Byron could be no system's slave; where Landor's extravagance precluded the sane appraisal of anything, Byron's excesses belonged to a less consistent character which included their antithesis. Landor's literary judgments are melodramatic; Byron's ostentatiously according to principle, and buttressed quite often by a display of irrelevant learning. And Byron, his fondness for invective apart, concerned himself less with pithy than with just appraisal. Much of his critical writing occurs between enthusiasm and disdain: 'Voltaire has even been termed a "shallow fellow", by some of the same school who called Dryden's Ode "a drunken song"; a *school* (as it is called, I presume, from their education being still incomplete) the whole of whose filthy trash of Epics, Excursions, etc. etc. etc. is not worth the two words in Zaire, "Vous pleurez", or a single speech of Tancred . . . ' Voltaire, he demonstrates in the notes to *Don Juan*, has been damned for a few errors of the type in which Bacon abounds. In the next note he points out a few errors committed by 'the justly celebrated Campbell'. Anstey could not have borrowed his leading characters from Smollett, because Anstey's Bath Guide was published in 1766 and Smollett's *Humphrey Clinker* in 1770, the latter being 'the only work from which Tabitha etc. could have been taken'. (But speaking of Campbell's poetry, Byron applies the unguent: Campbell and Rogers alone can be reproached with having written too little!)

There was a *Notes and Queries* streak in Byron that is often overlooked. He would never waste an opportunity for vituperation, but he had the uncommon habit of getting his facts right before he let fly. In matters of pure opinion too, he was much more moderate than has generally been assumed; only his fireworks are noticed. This comment on Macpherson's *Ossian* is typical of his responsible vein, but it comes from a note to *Hours of Idleness*:

. . . the merit of the work remains undisputed, though not without faults – particularly, in some parts, turgid and bombastic diction. . . .

Or take his appraisal of one of his favourite books, Mitford's *Greece*:

His great pleasure consists in praising tyrants, abusing Plutarch, spelling oddly, and writing quaintly; and what is strange, after all *his* is the best modern history of Greece in any language, and he is perhaps the best of all modern historians whatsoever. Having named his sins, it is but fair to state his virtues – learning, labour, research, wrath, and partiality. I call the latter virtues in a writer, because they make him write in earnest.

There is something suitable for Byron in that verdict; we could well borrow 'learning, labour, research, wrath and partiality' to describe the poet's own critical virtues.

He gets down to earth too, making a worthwhile point that has become trite only through long neglect of the condition he describes:

I wish to express, that we become tired of the task before we can comprehend the beauty; that we learn by rote before we can get by heart; that the freshness is worn away, and the future pleasure and advantage deadened and destroyed, by the didactic anticipation, at an age when we can neither feel nor understand the power of compositions which it requires an acquaintance with life, as well as Latin and Greek, to relish, or to reason upon. For the same reason, we can never be aware of the fulness of some of the finest passages of Shakespeare ('To be or not to be', for instance), from the habit of having them hammered into us at eight years old. . . . In some parts of the continent, young persons are taught from more common authors, and do not read the best classics till their maturity.

Elsewhere he comments more acidly on the same phenomenon:

Indeed, the public school penance of 'Long and Short' is enough to beget an antipathy to poetry for the residue of a man's life, and, perhaps, so far may be an advantage.

This 'well-founded horror of hexameters' accords with a subtler condition that he mentions in the notes to *Childe*

Harold. Commenting on a scholarly dispute, he says, 'I have quoted the passage merely to prove the similarity of style among the controversialists of all polished countries; London or Edinburgh could hardly parallel this Parisian ebullition'.

The type of cant which this evokes is well known. How odd, then, that Byron's preferences in poetry should have been Rogers, Crabbe and Campbell! The effete cataloguing of Rogers's *Italy*, the homespun dreariness of Crabbe, the thin patter of Campbell are not what we might expect. But if we probe a little, Byron's approval appears to be of secondary things. It is the geographer in Rogers that he likes, and his feeble sheen; it is not Crabbe's realism that he lauds ('he has got a coarse and impracticable subject') but his inheritance of Pope's manner without Pope's mentality; and his sight of Campbell is not very clear. There is a quotation in *Don Juan* from Campbell, and it goes like this:

> *Oh Love! in such a wilderness as this,*
> *Where transport and security entwine,*
> *Here is the empire of thy perfect bliss,*
> *And here thou art a god indeed divine.*

Now here is Byron's comment on this representative sample from 'Gertrude of Wyoming': 'The bard I quote from does not sing amiss, With the exception of the second line, For that same twining "transport and security" Are twisted to a phrase of some obscurity. The poet meant, no doubt, and thus appeals To the good sense and senses of mankind, The very thing which everybody feels, As all have found on trial, or may find, That no one likes to be disturb'd at meals or love.' Criticism is not taking place at all. Campbell's stanza is banal because it is stereotyped; and Byron's quip is on the same level as the inference by a present-day reader of a military pun in the second line – 'transport and security'. The note on this little joke gives the game away, and elucidates his view of Campbell:

'If anything could add to my opinion of the talents and true feeling of that gentleman, it would be his classical, honest, and triumphant defence of Pope, against the vulgar cant of the day, and its existing Grub Street'. The fact is that Byron praises these three for meaning well; he is fully alive to the solid innovation of Scott and Moore. He is torn between an eighteenth-century ideal of manner and a very practical appreciation of the easy poetry to be got from the exotic. To put it in another way, he wants to cash in on the vogue without prostituting his ideal. (One might think of Hemingway and Michener.) There were too many readers in Byron's day who – in T. S. Eliot's words – demanded 'of poetry a day-dream, or a metamorphosis of their own feeble desires and lusts, or what they believe(d) to be "intensity" of passion. . . .'

Byron's principal sympathy, it should be obvious, was with Pope's temperament only. There were times when, just as he played at literary criticism, Byron played with a poetic form. Somehow he had to integrate popular appeal, tough urbanity and a cavalier insensitivity to poetic forms and sounds. He is really a Frankenstein of the poetic instinct: a real Augustan would have demolished 'Gertrude of Wyoming', put the bastinado to Rogers's timid feet, and commended Crabbe for avoiding the exotic – for it is the exotic which, as in so many colour movies, blinds us luxuriantly to the absence of art. It is noteworthy that eventually Byron shelved all problems of form. He was too indolent and torn too many ways to be able to work out the apt form for his matter. That image of the concubine of snow recurs: he is anxious to dispose, somehow, somewhere.

But he did experiment. The trouble was that he did it without considering sufficiently the history of the forms he selected. He liked to improvise, too, and so neglected to explore his motives. He preferred to take someone else's word. There is an interesting note in this connexion which pertains to a line in *Hours of Idleness*: 'Soon as the gloaming spreads her waning shade'. The note reads like this:

As 'gloaming', the Scottish word for twilight, is far more poetical, and has been recommended by many eminent literary men, particularly by Dr Moore in his Letters to Burns, I have ventured to use it on account of its harmony.

A similar attitude shows up in the Preface to Cantos I and II of *Childe Harold*:

The stanza of Spenser, according to one of our most successful poets, admits of every variety. Dr Beattie makes the following observation: 'Not long ago, I began a poem in the style and stanza of Spenser, in which I propose to give full scope to my inclination, and be either droll or pathetic, descriptive or sentimental, tender or satirical, as the humour strikes me; for, if I mistake not, the measure which I have adopted admits equally of all these kinds of composition'. Strengthened in my opinion by such authority, and by some in the highest order of Italian poets, I shall make no apology for attempts at similar variations in the following composition; satisfied that if they are unsuccessful, their failure must be in the execution, rather than in the design, sanctioned by the practice of Ariosto, Thomson, and Beattie.

Surely, the unkind must have thought, this young man will do well. Cap in hand, he tries to forestall the examiners, but fails to ask whether any one of the worthy Dr Beattie's three sets of alternatives was intended to co-exist with the others. The young precisian is fulsome, and his expense of spirit significant. Introducing *The Corsair* he was to pronounce the Spenserian stanza 'perhaps too slow and too dignified for narrative'. But *Childe Harold* was hardly narrative, and the statement came with diminished force from one who confessed 'it is the measure most after my own heart'. He liked the stanza without testing it. Of the heroic couplet – 'perhaps the best adapted measure to our language'. he says that it 'is not the most popular measure certainly; but . . . I shall . . . take my chance once more with that versification, in which I have hitherto published nothing but compositions whose former circulation is part of my present, and will be of my future regret'. One might have expected him to think blank verse aptest for English; but Milton and the dramatists 'warn us from the rough and barren rock' of the iambic pentameter. And 'Scott, alone, of the present generation, has hitherto completely triumphed over the fatal facility of the octo-syllabic verse'. What of this fatality that Scott transcended? Certainly Byron's *The Bride of Abydos* is bad, not on account of any fatal quality in the measure, but because the stresses of colloquial speech have not been imposed upon the octosyllabic line. The octo-syllabics are awkward, and the poem's occasional pentameters are limping fustian. It is impatience that produces failures like the following:

> *Zuleika, mute and motionless,*
> *Stood like that statue of distress,*
> *When, her last hope for ever gone,*
> *The mother harden'd into stone:*
> *All in the maid that eye could see*
> *Was but a younger Niobé.*
>
> . . . . .
>
> *Not blind to fate, I see, where'er I rove,*
> *Unnumber'd perils – but one only love!*
> *Yet well my toils shall that fond breast repay,*
> *Though fortune frown, or falser friends betray.*

Byron, unfortunately, was incurious about the tension between spoken stress and count; and even in *Don Juan* he does not impose the one upon the other, but lets the one run riot. This is to the good of the choppy absurdities which are the essence of the poem. As so often with Byron, the experimental gestures (as with the *terza rima* in *The Prophecy of Dante*) are well-meant, but he is keener to be known to be experimenting than to define his problems clearly.

How are we to sum him up? He was fond of judging and of proclaiming, but he was not a literary critic. He wrote rather too easily. A popular entertainer with leanings to the erudite, he affected the pontifical insistence of Samuel Johnson almost as a *persona*. He idolized the eighteenth century and so wrote far too much in the couplet, when a moment's thought would have revealed the superiority, for his purposes, of any stanza form. (The varied ease of the *ottava rima* in *Morgante Maggiore* is a case in point: the urge to travesty has not broken through and the narrative is careful, melodious and richly woven.) He paid lip-service to 'regularity' and even sought to adapt his dramas to the 'unities': 'Conceiving that with any very distant departure from them, there may be poetry, but can be no drama.' Because 'Monk' Lewis advised him at Venice in 1817 that 'jealousy is an exhausted passion in the drama', he modified the action of *Marino Faliero*. In the preface to this play he adds that 'Sir William Drummond gave (him) nearly the same counsel'. It is one of the paradoxes of his nature that he explored his sources with scruple and thoroughness but, in the execution of the work, invoked inapt ideals, took the crassest advice and only rarely made up his own mind about problems of form. He wrote with mind averted, one eye on his public, the other on Pope's natty treadmill. A lustful man with a pedantic incubus, he got excited about one work only – *Don Juan*, the Byronic microcosm. He never related everything he touched to a single intellectual purpose. He was well equipped to carry his inconsistencies with him; so well equipped, in fact, that eventually he made them a virtue in their own right. In *Don Juan* he is a prisoner, but reconciled, playing the *farceur's* last brilliant hand, making the irresponsible irresistible all over again.

Chapter 3

THE FARCE WITH LANGUAGE

The first thing you have got to do, in reading Byron to purpose, is to remember his motto, 'Trust Byron'. You always may; and the more, that he takes some little pleasure at first in offending you. But all he says is true, nevertheless, though what worst of himself there is to tell, he insists upon at once; and what good there may be, mostly leaves you to find out.

(RUSKIN)

I

IF we agree that Byron's main skill is in comic verse although passages of serious meditation in *Childe Harold* are exquisitely pared, we see him developing in two ways. First, he gradually eliminates methods inappropriate to the rapidly maturing joker; and second, he appears to save what is eliminated for later second-hand duty in his knacker's yard of a comic poem. Like the uncertain critic, he puts his doubtful ideas in apostrophes and leaves to the reader the job of assigning and assessing. There are parts of *Don Juan* which can be taken seriously in themselves. But in the context they become exploited for idiocy or symbol, according to the reader's inference: the romantic and military episodes represent conscious parody of a rejected mode or, more subtly, the fate – in an uncaring world – of any high aspiration. These things are not made clear, and there is, within the Byronic poetic code, no reason why they should be. The ringmaster, polished, blasé, has a hired smile, but no explanations. He offers runes and charms, which are intended to do very practical things – to make us laugh or tremble. And Byron's interjections are not from him in person, but are examples presented by him of someone interrupting.

They are part of the act. Even the rude allusions to contemporaries strike those familiar with the other poems as cool facsimiles of habitual tricks. By the time of *Don Juan*, Byron was able to present himself for his interest as an object, and this without feeling implicated at all. In other words, a complete abdication of the responsible mind confers opportunities for utter farce – just like canny Baudelaire watching himself from the ceiling.

Towards this abdication, Byron manœuvred himself only very unsteadily. The romantic themes – Corsair, Giaour, Siege, Prisoner, Curse, Bride, Island, the riders, escapers and avengers – pressed themselves upon him; and it was only later that he saw them as mere specimens. He rang the changes on these themes and tossed them off in couplets of eight or ten syllables, or in a mixture of couplet and stanza. His recourse to the couplet was near-instinctive; one suspects that he liked the couplet because its rhyming demands did not sustain themselves beyond two lines. This suited the grasshopper mind that leapt from one delight (or incongruity) to the next. And his experiments with a mixed method look more like the gestures of a negligent change-seeking than the effort to devise a complex form. 'And now for a change . . .' seems to be the drift of his mind: the sudden shortening of the line and incursions into stanza are demanded by no switch in mood, subject or time. They are not introduced with some larger symmetry in mind; no musical pattern is attempted; they give relief without seeming to give the added sense of interpretation that Shelley and Wordsworth manage. As Byron said on several occasions, 'regularity' attracted him, but not to the point of obsession. Of the planned irregularity implicit in a complex structure, he said nothing. It was the pursuit of novelty that took him to the *terza rima* for *The Prophecy of Dante*. Subject to all manner of fads, he yet never quite got to the point of determining the excellences and disadvantages of a particular poetic form. He hit on the *ottava rima* by accident[1]; for the translation of *Morgante Maggiore* is good writing in the stanza, but not the supreme style, of *Don Juan* – good writing far from comic and in the vein of the couplet romances.

All this, of course, is not to vote him blind to form but to specify his blindnesses to the subtler means of articulation. No one blind to form could have exploited the Spenserian stanza as thoroughly as he did in *Childe Harold* for purposes reflective, lyrical, descriptive and even narrative. But *Childe Harold* is so full of the actual world, 'the labyrinth of external objects', that the dreamy, flatulent stanza looks and sounds inapt. What might have been crisp reporting declines into a languid pageant:

> *All things are here of him; from the black pines,*
> *Which are his shade on high, and the loud roar*
> *Of torrents, where he listeneth, to the vines*
> *Which slope his green path downward to the shore,*
> *Where the bow'd waters meet him, and adore,*
> *Kissing his feet with murmurs; and the wood,*
> *The covert of old trees, with trunks all hoar,*
> *But light leaves, young as joy, stands where it stood,*
> *Offering to him, and his, a populous solitude.*

This needs tightening up: he is cementing units together; he has not set the whole in motion; the language is otiose. He is filling the space, whereas in the following stanza from *Don Juan* the images protrude from their places; and the last thing to come to mind is that the poet ever had a bare structure to fill in:

> *Turkey contains no bells, and yet men dine;*
> *And Juan and his friend, albeit they heard*

---

[1] He says that *ottava rima*'s possibilities for satirical burlesque were made clear when he read *The Monks and the Giants* (1817) by J. H. Frere, country gentleman, diplomatist and translator of Aristophanes. Frere had tried to imitate in English the satirical Italian epic.

No Christian knoll to table, saw no line
Of lackeys usher to the feast prepared,
Yet smelt roast-meat, beheld a huge fire shine,
And cooks in motion with their clean arms bared,
And gazed around them to the left and right,
With the prophetic eye of appetite.

This is immaculate, from the sounding lunge of the first line to the splendidly subdued, suddenly formalized wit of the last. The tone is euphoric, all sounding brass, bellows and sensually brash. Between the phrases there is much activity; but the stanza describes inactivity. The aim is to catalogue, and there is no shortage of objects. The method is visual: not to present objects with a superimposed rôle culled from the familiarly poetic, but to keep the reader's eye on the objects, and especially on the close-up that carries a climate – 'And cooks in motion with their clean arms bared'.

Childe Harold was popular. But the Byronic comedy could have come in its place, as this *Epitaph on John Adams, of Southwell* suggests:

(A CARRIER, WHO DIED OF DRUNKENNESS)
John Adams lies here, of the parish of Southwell,
A Carrier who carried his can to his mouth well:
He carried so much, and he carried so fast,
He could carry no more – so was carried at last;
For, the liquor he drank, being too much for one,
He could not carry off, – so he's now carri-on.

The date of this composition is September 1807. The puns that gesture at us, the callousness of the folksy fun, the feminine rhymes and, indeed, the subject itself, all look forward. June of 1810 saw the birth of a firework in the same ludicrous kind:

THE FARCE WITH LANGUAGE

Oh how I wish that an embargo
Had kept in port the good ship Argo!
Who, still unlaunch'd from Grecian docks,
Had never pass'd the Azure rocks;
But now I fear her trip will be a
Damn'd business for my Miss Medea, etc. etc.

It is possible that the Spenserian stanza distracted Byron from
his gift for irreverence. True, that stanza assisted into being
some of the most elegant and unfanciful elegiac writing he ever
did:

They keep his dust in Arqua, where he died;
The mountain-village where his latter days
Went down the vale of years; and 'tis their pride –
An honest pride – and let it be their praise,
To offer to the passing stranger's gaze
His mansion and his sepulchre; both plain
And venerably simple, such as raise
A feeling more accordant with his strain
Than if a pyramid form'd his monumental fane.

But even here, the feeling for words in 'venerably simple' has
to lapse into the tedious coda that follows. Byron would have
written a *Childe Harold* anyway, but with a different stanza
would have written less fustian. When he attempts to be
sententious with a worldly slant, the stanza robs the utterance
of point and trenchancy:

Not much he kens, I ween, of woman's breast,
Who thinks that wanton thing is won by sighs;
What careth she for hearts when once possess'd?
Do proper homage to thine idol's eyes;
But not too humbly, or she will despise

Thee and thy suit, though told in moving tropes:
Disguise ev'n tenderness, if thou art wise;
Brisk Confidence still best with woman copes:
Pique her and soothe in turn, soon Passion crowns thy hopes.

The squib is damp. We have only to compare with a stanza on a similar theme, from *Don Juan*:

Alas! Worlds fall – and woman, since she fell'd
The world (as, since that history, less polite
Than true, hath been a creed so strictly held),
Has not yet given up the practice quite.
Poor thing of usages! coerced, compell'd,
Victim when wrong, and martyr oft when right,
Condemn'd to child-bed, as men for their sins
Have shaving too entail'd upon their chins, –

The first passage is pure Polonius, dustily venerable for the logic of its advice, but ordinary and lacking in edge. The altogether too facile personification in the penultimate line makes the whole performance sound ancient and patronizing. In contrast, the passage from *Don Juan* is more realistic and more trenchant. The advice is not better (one imagines), but the style is tauter, and the end-couplet shows up the true paralysis of its counterpart in the other passage. The quatrains in *Don Juan* are perpetrated with great gusto and equal discipline:

For over-warmth, if false, is worse than truth;
If true, 'tis no great lease of its own fire;
For no one, save in very early youth,
Would like (I think) to trust all to desire. . . .

The first four lines of every stanza leap into activity, bristling with matter and controversy. The same cannot be said about many stanzas in *Childe Harold*: the majority sag under the weight, not only of reflective melancholy, but of difficulties peculiar to the stanza chosen.

Consider, for instance, the rhyme pattern: ABABBCBCC. The stanza begins with a simple ABAB quatrain; but the fifth line repeats the B, and so makes a couplet in the wrong place: wrong because the couplet clinches, dismisses and yet goes on sounding in the mind's ear. Next, a new rhyme C is introduced, and this has to be plangent enough to muffle the reverberations of the couplet. But no sooner has this new rhyme C done its work, if it can within the dictates of available words, than the couplet rhyme is newly evoked, and the stanza concluded by a couplet on C. Thus, what is plangent can only be subdued by using a rhyme which, used three times in four lines, must not be too heavy itself. Needless to say, there are no feminine rhymes in *Childe Harold*. The problem is onerous: can the C rhyme muffle without obtruding too much? Even the addition in the last line of extra syllables cannot keep the C rhymes far enough apart. And, worst of all, the final couplet can contain no surprise or freak, because its sound has already been announced in the sixth line. This is a stanza, then, of unfortunate strata. Evoking the couplet's tidy despatch, it at the same time slumps into monotony towards the end. Perfect for Spenser's timeless vista, it gets Byron into phrases and torpors he does not require. The following will serve to demonstrate.

> *Oh Time! the beautifier of the dead,*
> *Adorner of the ruin, comforter*
> *And only healer when the heart hath bled;*   3
> *Time! the corrector where our judgments err,*
> *The test of truth, love – sole philosopher,*
> *For all beside are sophists – from thy thrift,*   6
> *Which never loses though it doth defer –*
> *Time, the avenger! unto thee I lift*
> *My hands, and eyes, and heart, and crave of thee a gift:*

He weakens the pervasive B rhyme (comforter, err, philosopher, defer) and thereby the couplet (4-5). He tries to fix our attention on the beginnings of the lines, and so is compelled into three rather jejune apostrophes (Oh Time! | Time! | Time, the avenger!) Avoidance of the plangent entails the melodramatic, and so monopolizes his attention that he lets in the unfortunate anticipations and echoes (beautifier, adorner, healer, corrector, never, avenger) of the 'err' rhyme. So does care blind itself! And he tries desperately in the last line to disturb the flow of the couplet.

The overall impression given is one of exhaustion. A graceful stanza will seem to exhaust its content just as it ends. But the exhaustion here is not that of a thorough working-out, is not the stop from completion; it is the result of over-exertion for secondary purposes. Not only that; the stanza's exhaustion promotes its own fault: the exertions were to combat the dulling rhymes that give a tired sound; but the exertion in those apostrophes, the dashes that amplify or display (as well as keeping us lively) merely intensify the fatigue. There is no brooking the Spenserian stanza: the remedies it seems to demand merely aggravate the complaint. It sets up, as it were, a closed circuit of sounds in ninety-two syllables: they echo one another too quickly for too long. If you are writing timelessly, nothing is better. Other sounds, and an attendant world of other times, seem excluded. A dead-end of sonority recurs throughout *Childe Harold*, relieved only by a few songs. The poem is worth studying for the variety of Byron's efforts to evade the dangers of the stanza. He breaks up the lines with dashes and commas; works hard at enjambements; exclaims, invokes, slips into italics, and does his best to prevent the central couplet from being self-sufficient.

All of which betokens some sensitivity to form; that is, enough to see the pitfalls, but too little to make him switch forms rather than seize an immense opportunity for impro-

vising. In *Don Juan* he breaks up the stanza-pattern, not to foil
its nature, but to show off: 'see what I can do with this stanza
short of breaking it!' And all this because in *The Vision of
Judgment*, *Beppo*, *Morgante Maggiore* and *Don Juan* he is sure of
his grasp on the form; sure, too, that his purposes are such that
the stanza cannot let him down:

> *The spirits were in neutral space, before*
> *The gate of heaven; like eastern thresholds is*
> *The place where Death's grand cause is argued o'er,*
> *And souls despatch'd to that world or to this;*
> *And therefore Michael and the other wore*
> *A civil aspect: though they did not kiss,*
> *Yet still between his Darkness and his Brightness*
> *There pass'd a mutual glance of great politeness.*

That, from *The Vision of Judgment*, is confident and creative
writing: 'neutral space' is a rich and sophisticated concept; the
remainder is suffused with it, and needs no extra piquancy;
both scene and tone are set. The last two lines are original: it
is exciting to find a commonplace 'mutual glance of great
politeness' passing between the two elevated and resounding
personages. The wit arrives through preposterous misapplica-
tion – or, if there is nothing amiss in the application, through
preposterous display of the apposite. Opposing counsel on the
brink of hell . . . the wit is in the magnification of the glance;
for to be applied amiss or otherwise, it has to seem magnified
for the magniloquence to take effect.

But Byron can achieve another reduction to or magnification
into absurdity. This is done again by a combination in the
couplet; the stanza is from *Beppo*:

> *But saving this, you may put on whate'er*
> *You like by way of doublet, cape, or cloak,*
> *Such as in Monmouth-street, or in Rag Fair,*
> *Would rig you out in seriousness or joke;*

And even in Italy such places are,
With prettier name in softer accents spoke,
For, bating Covent Garden, I can hit on
No place that's called 'Piazza' in Great Britain.

The mundane serious is lightened but not transfigured by the madcap rhyme; it simply assumes its place among the absurd; it becomes an item, laughable through affiliation, an object not of, but just sponsored by, ridicule. When the cushion we sit on squeaks, we are supposed to laugh. Similarly, when Byron digs up 'Great Britain' as a rhyme, we laugh because it is an unexpected breach of congruity. There is daring ('go on, ask me another! defy me to rhyme with it!') together with a loose assumption of our sympathy. The triumph is in finding a rhyme; the concept within the rhyme-word is not as important here as it is in E. E. Cummings's couplet:

> *here is little Effie's head*
> *whose brains are made of gingerbread*

'Effie' is vaguely undignified, and 'gingerbread' in this context is unfamiliar. The silly, allied with the sinister in a vague way, erupts into cosy horror. This is also Byron's method: rhyme is of the utmost importance.

Rhyme, at its most primitive, was an emphatic and remembering device. For the known, it could almost magically elicit from the unknown a twin. Rhyme is company, confidence, safety, enclosure, a shape, a wonderful short arm of coincidence. Its essence is that of a travelling companion, heading the same way in an adjacent slot. It has two phases; 'wild' and 'child' rhyming together merely create a framework; and to our awareness of the similarity we add little care for the conjoined ideas. But if 'Adorer' elicits 'there before her', our sense of framework is flooded with a sense of something on the level of thought. Usually, however, rhyme is expected to supply a reassuring framework in sound. The rhyme may be ingenious and hard-worked-for, but it is not expected to draw more than a token aural and certainly not a mental attention to itself. Thus there is, for example, a specialized inattention to the rhyme words in a hymn: as long as they supply the requisite framework, they are hardly noticed. But the words of a psalm are likely to strike home, merely because they are not fulfilling structural functions of an obvious type.

The structural unity of the psalm depends on repetitions; and if we sense form developing rather than shape superinduced, it is because the psalm proceeds by building on itself. Certain components turn out to be keystones. But we realize this only on looking back. In the hymn, on the other hand, the pleasure we get from the form is one of anticipation. After thirty words of a psalm, we may still be in the dark as to its pattern. After one stanza of a hymn, we can guess fairly accurately. In the one, form is always developing; in the other, it is prescribed in detail. And so, in a sense, the psalm is capable of greater surprise: its power of *dénouement* exceeds that of the hymn. repetition is the psalm's principle; the hymn is caged. The psalm is (in R. P. Blackmur's phrase) expressive form, such as we find attempted in D. H. Lawrence's poems, Pound's *Cantos*, Hart Crane's *The Bridge* and Carlos Williams's *Paterson*. And expressive here means unexacting: repetition is the instinctive device of the person exultant, hysterical or emphatic. There is a minimum of artful manipulation. As Marianne Moore says in 'The Past and the Present', 'Hebrew poetry is prose with a sort of heightened consciousness'. Ecstasy affords the occasion and expediency determines the form. To Miss Moore – herself a fastidious constructor of patterns that *expose* words at special angles – Hebrew poetry is one type of emphatic pattern. Pattern enlivens material; too complex a pattern becomes idiosyncratic. Too simple a pattern (like that of D. H. Lawrence's poetry) deprives the writer of persuasiveness.

61

Byron's persuasiveness is at its best in his couplets. In the *ottava rima* (ABABABCC) the first two rhymes are over-worked but are swiftly despatched – at full tilt as it were – by the new rhyme of the couplet. The stanza appears to turn inside out at the instigation of a freakish bond: condition/circumcision, Bashaw/sire-in-law, patience/provocations, sparing/cheese-paring, Italy/prettily, harlot/scarlet, etc. But this process depends too on the ideas expressed in the couplet: the point being that two such ill-matched concepts could be integrated into a statement both coherent and apposite:

> *Judges in very formidable ermine*
> *Were there, with brows that did not much invite*
> *The accused to think their lordships would determine*
> *His cause by leaning much from might to right:*
> *Bishops, who had not left a single sermon;*
> *Attorneys-general, awful to the sight,*
> *As hinting more (unless our judgments warp us)*
> *Of the 'Star Chamber' than of 'Habeas Corpus'.*

The couplet is well enough integrated to disturb the preceding pomp and circumstance – already ruffled in this stanza by a few extra syllables. But superfluous cleverness is at a minimum here; the disrespect is of a mildly relevant kind. The early scene is not travestied, but winked at – a joke among men. But the following is much more gratuitous:

> *Unless when qualified with thee, Cogniac!*
> *Sweet Naïad of the Phlegethontic rill!*
> *Ah! why the liver wilt thou thus attack,*
> *And make, like other nymphs, thy lovers ill?*
> *I would take refuge in weak punch, but rack*
> *(In each sense of the word), whene'er I fill*
> *My mild and midnight beakers to the brim,*
> *Wakes me next morning with its synonym.*

THE FARCE WITH LANGUAGE

But the Byronic concept of *Don Juan* as a rag-bag of interesting exhibits reduces itself to an occasional self-indulgent absurdity. The author has his readers only the least bit in mind; and where simulated indiscretion, self-conscious intrusions, mock-confidences and outlandish polysyllables only augment his dazzling and pleasing disrespect for us, the following piece can hardly be accommodated into even a 'versified Aurora Borealis':

> But here is one prescription out of many:
> 'Sodae sulphat. 3vj. 3fs. Mannae optim.
> Aq. fervent. f. ℥ ifs. 3ij. tinct. Sennae
> Haustus' (and here the surgeon came and cupp'd him),
> 'R.Pulv. Com. gr.iij. Ipecacuanhae'
> (With more beside if Juan had not stopp'd 'em).
> 'Bolus Potassae Sulphuret. sumendus,
> Et haustus ter in die capiendus.'

This is the world of objects adapted for ends of fun. It always suited Byron to play collector with things and people. He was always vacillating between subduing both by the over-endowments of his personality and body, and becoming the man of stone who has no needs. He is all elimination, whether he eliminates his own surplus feeling or the objects upon which feeling might be directed. It would not be unfair to read many of his poems as animated bestiaries, although the worldly wisdom that he dispensed cannot apply very widely:

> There's also nightly, to the uninitiated,
> A peril – not indeed like love or marriage,
> But not the less for this to be depreciated:
> It is – I meant and mean not to disparage
> The show of virtue even in the vitiated –
> It adds an outward grace unto their carriage –
> But to denounce the amphibious sort of harlot,
> Couleur de rose, *who's neither white nor scarlet.*

Often he seems, as here, enclosed in a wisdom all of his own, which applies little to the lives of others but which he enjoys formulating stylishly. The Byronic nostrum is too specialized.

When he is writing narrative, he mutilates least and so appeals to a wide audience which has not to appraise his ideas or respond to his farce and introspection. Here is a stanza of pure action from *Morgante Maggiore*:

> *Morgante at a venture shot an arrow,*
> *Which pierced a pig precisely in the ear,*
> *And pass'd unto the other side quite thorough;*
> *So that the boar, defunct, lay tripp'd up near.*
> *Another, to revenge his fellow farrow,*
> *Against the giant rush'd in fierce career,*
> *And reached the passage with so swift a foot,*
> *Morgante was not now in time to shoot.*

Nothing in this is superfluous. The quality of action is accurately felt: the casual shot, the ironically precise way it struck, the sudden stumble (which we infer), the almost immediate charge of the second beast, the man with the beast upon him – this last perfectly conveyed by those bated-breath monosyllables of the accomplished story-teller. The stanza fits its purpose without overlap or prompting mere structural invention. But the sharpness of his eye alone was sufficient to give great pleasure to his reader. Take this excerpt from his journal: he responds to the world of sense with extraordinary perspective and avidity:

Came home *solus* – very high wind – lightning – moonshine – solitary stragglers muffled in cloaks – women in masks – white houses – clouds hurrying over the sky, like spilt milk blown out of the pail – altogether very poetical. It is still blowing hard – the tiles flying, and the house rocking – rain splashing – lightning flashing – quite a fine Swiss Alpine evening, and the sea roaring in the distance.

When he went to an execution in Rome, he took an opera glass; he never forgot having seen Shelley's brains seethe and bubble in the cranium when the corpse was burned; he insisted on sampling the sea-water which had drowned Shelley and Williams, and was violently sick as a result. It would be easy to accumulate further instances of this intoxicating curiosity; it seemed as if he could never devour enough of 'the indubitable world of sense'. Perhaps the voracity came from a need for reassurance; perhaps it was a means of possession and was the only device to keep him from indifference. It is difficult to explain fully the shifts of so complex a personality. But from the various evidences of guilt we might conclude that a lust for life degenerated into mere sensation-seeking, and that Byron affected indifference merely to preserve his self-respect. The ancient debauchee, as he said in *Don Juan*, likes sour fruit to stir his 'veins' salt tides, As acids rouse a dormant alkali'. At the execution, he had noted 'the *masqued* priests; the half-naked executioners; the bandaged criminals; the black Christ and his banner; the scaffold; the soldiery; the slow procession, and the quick rattle and fall of the axe; the splash of the blood, and the ghastliness of the exposed heads. . . .' The experience made him quiver, left him hot and thirsty. Then follows a significant comment on 'how dreadfully soon things grow indifferent'. In order to avert indifference, must the satiate appetite seek out gross and violent stimulants? It is a nice dilemma, and one which Byron resolved only by going off, not ungrudgingly, to help rid Greece of the Turks. He died before he could achieve much. But his dying words suggest a victory over indifference at least: 'Poor Greece – poor town – my poor servants. *Io lascio qualche cosa di caro nel mondo*. I am leaving behind me something dear in the world.'

II

In one sense *Childe Harold* and *Don Juan* constitute opposite ways out of this dilemma of satiety; ways not to be described solely in terms of the behaviour illustrated in those poems, but pursued into the minutiae of poetic texture. The bull-fight in the first canto of *Childe Harold* is vividly described – over-described, perhaps – as if Byron feared that economy of means entailed inadequacy of result. Spread over seven stanzas, the description seems clogged; but a stanza taken in isolation displays without excess the skill of the embalmer:

> *Where his vast neck just mingles with the spine,*
> *Sheathed in his form the deadly weapon lies.*
> *He stops – he starts – disdaining to decline :*
> *Slowly he falls, amidst triumphant cries,*
> *Without a groan, without a struggle dies.*
> *The decorated car appears – on high*
> *The corse is piled – sweet sight for vulgar eyes –*
> *Four steeds that spurn the rein, as swift as shy,*
> *Hurl the dark bulk along, scarce seen in dashing by.*

The Spenserian stanza is specially suitable when passion is spent; its special merit is that it sets everything behind thick glass; the sound, as is so often noticed, interferes with activities within the stanza. Throughout *Childe Harold* imagery already current in poetry is carefully mounted and made seductively visible at two removes. The first interference is the hero's resolutely magniloquent world-sadness; the second is the dreaming stanza. What comes through is unmistakable, but not quite of the daily world – rather like technicolour on the curved screen. But, compared with *Don Juan*, there is a fastidious concern for presentation. The imagery of *Don Juan* is smugly up to date (galvanism and all that), heterogeneous and rather scrambled. There is little supervision. The unruly elements are bundled in and allowed to conflict. The phrasing is contorted and the tone is erratic. Even the decorum of satire is shattered. This, the poem seems to say, is how life is; and life is not to be taken in tablet form as this poem is. The poet makes no effort to ensure congruity but indulges in it when he fancies:

> Haidée was Nature's bride, and knew not this:
> Haidée was Passion's child, born where the sun
> Showers triple light, and scorches even the kiss
> Of his gazelle-eyed daughters; she was one
> Made but to love, to feel that she was his
> Who was her chosen: what was said or done
> Elsewhere was nothing. She had nought to fear,
> Hope, care, nor love beyond, – her heart beat here.

But the simple charm of that soon yields in the next stanza to:

> . . . even Conscience, too, has a tough job
> To make us understand each good old maxim,
> So good – I wonder Castlereagh don't tax 'em.

Another difference between the two poems is that *Childe Harold* teems with things seen sharply and devotedly. *Don Juan* is mostly enumeration with little effort to see. Where *Childe Harold* is lengthily philosophical, the other poem is aphoristic. *Childe Harold* is meant to persuade; the poet attends to the reader, explains, repeats, underlines. *Don Juan* tries to bounce the reader into assent. Take it or leave it, shouts the poet, sticking out his head while he works the marionettes with his hands. The rhythms are ragged, the vocabulary is wide but is used impatiently. The similes are fantastic:

> She stood a moment as a Pythoness
> Stands on her tripod, agonised, and full
> Of inspiration gather'd from distress,
> When all the heart-strings like wild horses pull
> The heart asunder. . . .

There are excursions into what modern taste might call the idiom of the music-hall. We are presented with an incongruous vagueness susceptible of lewd or demeaning interpretations:

> *At length she rose up, and began to walk*
> *Slowly along the room, but silent still,*
> *And her brow clear'd, but not her troubled eye;*
> *The wind was down but still the sea ran high.*
>
> *He likewise could be most things to all women,*
> *Without the coxcombry of certain she men.*

The poet unbends to doggerel, tries to keep his couplets sober during narrative, but for the most part pushes the feminine rhyme as far as it will go. In *Morgante Maggiore* the narrative permits only a quarter of the final couplets to have feminine rhymes. But in *Beppo* the tally is over half, and in *Don Juan* over three-quarters. This feminine rhyme is variously used – for flourish, moral and burlesque; but its main function is to add a note of giddiness. The flippancy that Lady Blessington reproved in Byron serves, in *Don Juan*, to make frivolous what might not otherwise be bearable. At least, that is how Byron externalizes the private habit in the following:

> *O Time! why dost not pause? Thy scythe, so dirty*
> *With rust, should surely cease to hack and hew.*
> *Reset it: shave more smoothly, also slower,*
> *If but to keep thy credit as a mower.*
>
> *'Tis strange the mind, that very fiery particle,*
> *Should let itself be snuff'd out by an article.*

The method is simple; everything is submitted to the same requirement: it must be interesting, even if it is so only because it is funny. This at once widens Byron's scope and lowers his tone. Nothing is sacred, not even the cherished themes of earlier success, not even afflictions made light of, not even eminence, the proscribed, the martyred, not even valour or scandal. Nothing is transfigured, either; the items are made to consort together in the ludicrous dance of the stanzas. Hapless under the aspect of fatuity they rattle into view and, when they have gone, appear to have been the merest pretexts for the sententious joker who follows:

> *I think you'll find from many a family picture,*
> *That daughters of such mothers as may know*
> *The world by experience rather than by lecture,*
> *Turn out much better for the Smithfield Show*
> *Of vestals brought into the marriage mart,*
> *Than those bred up by prudes without a heart.*

But, of course, even the sententious is put through the hoop, and it is the neatness of the statement, rather than its burden, that extorts approval:

> *Though several also keep their perpendicular*
> *Like poplars, with good principles for roots;*
> *Yet many have a method more reticular –*
> *'Fishers for men', like sirens with soft lutes:*
> *For talk six times with the same single lady,*
> *And you may get the wedding dresses ready.*

But the cleverest performances depend more on Byron's knack for summary than on the summary quality of aphorism. The very remote observer sees a pattern which looks almost the same thing as the interpretation to be placed upon it. And Byron, with his power of epitome, his ability (like Auden's) to make the detail generic, his habit of compressing without impairing, tends always to generalize observation to the point of abstract knowledge:

> *But whether fits, or wits, or harpsichords,*
> *Theology, fine arts, or finer stays,*

May be the baits for gentlemen or lords   3
With regular descent, in these our days,
The last year to the new transfers its hoards;
New vestals claim men's eyes with the same praise   6
Of 'elegant' et cetera, in fresh batches –
All matchless creatures, and yet bent on matches.

There are some pleasing relationships between these words: 'fits' elicits 'wits'; the shading of the word 'fine' is piquantly done; 'harpsichords' is a nicely preposterous misalliance with 'lords', and the apparent paradox in the last line has something of the conjuror's bland exposition – 'nothing in my hands, nothing up my sleeves' – and yet, what isn't, suddenly is. The words in the first three lines vigorously proclaim their separateness within grammar's brief contract. They sound different, and the homonyms disturb each other's currents. The weakness of the stanza begins with 'in these our days': the effort towards a larger gesture makes the texture featureless until the last line. To read the stanza and omit lines 4 and 5 is to gain in pungency what is lost in respite. The stanza is made up of two series of thrusts before and after those two lines; and the individual reader has to decide for himself whether a ceaseless thrusting (which Byron's couplets sustain in *English Bards*) is tedious, and needs a contrast – a spell of self-collection and survey. What is indisputable is Byron's constant effort at a conspectus of his own imagination – sometimes to the detriment of detail, sometimes to an immense gain in universality:

> *I call such things transmission; for there is*
> *A floating balance of accomplishment,*
> *Which forms a pedigree from Miss to Miss,*
> *According as their minds or backs are bent.*
> *Some waltz; some draw; some fathom the abyss*
> *Of metaphysics.*" . . .

The gain here is in the second, third and fourth lines: the opening generalization is so precisely made that it makes the ensuing particulars look false. But the excellence of statement is not peculiar to poetic expression; it belongs to educated utterance in a context of forbearance and irony. And it is Byron's awareness of his own double motive which enables him to scout the trite generality and so make his statements in his own way:

> Perhaps you'll have a letter from the mother,
> To say her daughter's feelings are trepann'd;
> Perhaps you'll have a visit from the brother,
> All strut, and stays, and whiskers, to demand
> What 'your intentions are?' . . .

'Trepanned' makes the passage Byron's and 'the brother' ironic, towards that person and to the *type* he evokes. The style of *Don Juan* helped Byron to say all he wanted; it did not confine him. And in saying what he wanted, he lost a good deal, including the knack of sustaining a lyric without self-consciousness, and any viewpoint but that of exhibitor – as the following reveals:

> She was not violently lively, but
> Stole on your spirit like a May-day breaking;
> Her eyes were not too sparkling, yet, half-shut,
> They put beholders in a tender taking;
> She look'd (this simile's quite new) just cut
> From marble. . . .

The first line is perhaps tolerable; the second too evocative of a stereotyped trope rentable from the Poets' Club; the third acceptable – the brilliant discord that brings ecstasy nearer home; the fourth fantastically archaic like an old-fashioned piano accompanying a vistavision talkie; and the fifth, spell-breaking as a radio commercial, but the epitome of Byron's ventriloquistic method. 'Cut from marble', the poem says: but perhaps we are intended to think not of sculptors but of cheese.

The method of *Don Juan* has another aspect: the exhibitionist displaces the scrutineer. And what at first glance may seem close observation is really An Exercise in the Mode of Detailed Knowledge – a very different thing from a familiar object caught perhaps for the first time in a rare phase. Compare the following passages, for instance:

> *And for the effeminate* villegiatura –
> *Rife with more horns than hounds* – *she hath the chase,*
> *So animated that it might allure a*
> *Saint from his beads to join the jocund race*. . . .

> *It is a far cry from the 'queen full of jewels'*
> *and the beau with the muff,*
> *from the gilt coach shaped like a perfume-bottle,*
> *to the conjunction of the Monongahela and the Allegheny*. . . .

These passages are by Byron and Marianne Moore respectively, and in them the writers deploy original items both knowingly and elegantly. This is the poetry of peculiarity, the lyricism of hoarding – written, as it were, by squirrels of exquisite perception and sensibility. And this is really all that Byron gives us. There is nothing in his work that resembles Marianne Moore's 'swan, with swart blind look askance / and gondoliering legs', which is a unique perception, re-making the seen, exposing the new in the familiar.

It is very easy to identify the exotic with the poetic and the lavish with the artistic: that was the burden of Julien Benda's *Belphégor* (1918); it is the stock indentification of Hollywood; it is the identification which affiliates Marlowe, Leconte de Lisle, Sir Walter Scott and Doughty. Poetry, as Stefan Georg insisted with continual vehemence, is not journalism. True, poetry needs objects which are inserted as *exempla* ((HURRY UP PLEASE ITS TIME; Carlos Williams's NO DOGS ALLOWED IN THIS PARK; Pound's use in his *Cantos* of excerpts from the Adams-Jefferson letters), and present-day taste is accustomed to such devices. But it is the context that decides the quality of the insertion. Marianne Moore's great skill is in catching things as they move and develop; it is when she is doing this that her sinewy accuracy shows most. Of course, if you want to be accurate, sooner or later you have to steal, import and quote. But the obligation remains: to integrate or transmute.

In this respect Byron falls sadly short. He is content to evoke the familiar or to photograph the exotic. His equipment and technique are superb; but he fails, as the camera fails, to re-create the object contemplated. How many passages in Byron prompt us to exclaim at the originality of his vision? There are occasional flashes in his journal – a mountain torrent recalls 'the *tail* of a white horse streaming in the wind' – but the poetry takes objects at their face value, presenting them in straight-forward manner. The flights of fancy are the usual ones – nothing idiosyncratic there; and the general tone is that of a man both lively and articulate, both intelligent and open-eyed, but with a commonplace eye:

> *A mighty mass of brick, and smoke, and shipping,*
> *Dirty and dusky, but as wide as eye*
> *Could reach, with here and there a sail just skipping*
> *In sight, then lost amidst the forestry*
> *Of masts; a wilderness of steeples peeping*
> *On tiptoe through their sea-coal canopy;*
> *A huge, dun cupola, like a foolscap crown*
> *On a fool's head – and there is London Town.*

'On tiptoe' is the only extravagance here, and that hardly fits into this man-to-man poetry. The irreverence of the 'foolscap crown' is Byron's way of a graceful exit. Compared with the following passage from Hemingway, the stanza looks overdone. But the motives of both passages are similar: the celebration of those items into which one need not inquire.

He sat on the logs, smoking, drying in the sun, the sun warm on his back, the river shallow ahead entering the woods, curving into the woods, shallows, light glittering, big water-smooth rocks, cedars along the bank and white birches, the logs warm in the sun, smooth to sit on, without bark, gray to the touch. . . .

There are no clichés in this passage; but there are no tropes either. Hemingway's imagery is of an elementary sort: it is everything which is not principally devoted to the main-tenance of syntax. Hemingway extolls by accumulating, by refusing to articulate the relationships between words, by removing a dimension. In some ways he does what the Spenserian stanza does rather better: he banishes time, nexus and perspective. But the parallels do not stop there. Robert Jordan, who once taught at Montana University, is not far removed from Childe Harold, or *For Whom the Bell Tolls* from Byron's poem. Byron's language is more high-flown, more overtly poetical; but the pageant of the bleeding heart closely resembles that of the heart that is suppressed. Man suffers; nature does not.

Byron, like Hemingway, shows an intense love of colour, fragrance and sound. They both present nature as a commodity delicious and mystical. It is the fixed element in their cos-mologies, and is not to be inquired into too curiously:

> *The difficult air of the iced mountain's top,*
> *Where the birds dare not build, nor insect's wing*
> *Flit o'er the herbless granite. . . .*

That comes from *Manfred*. Byron does not inquire, but that does not prevent him from being vivid and from handling language voluptuously: 'herbless granite'. And this incurious quality of Byron's imagery makes it very suitable for drama and narrative. In drama it is the suffusing force of an image that is important; the audience has no time to pore over the text. In narrative, even what is descriptive cannot be complex. Byron's language is best when direct:

> ... *Men may,*
> *Even aged men, be, or appear to be,*
> *Sires of a hundred sons, but cannot kindle*
> *An atom of their ancestors from earth.*

It is the last line here which makes the passage carry. Another passage from the same play, *The Two Foscari*, shows Byron's non-analytical imagery at its best. (Dramatic writing, even when not intended for the stage, gave him the best pretext for bareness.)

> ... *How many a time have I*
> *Cloven with arm still lustier, breast more daring,*
> *The wave all roughen'd; with a swimmer's stroke*
> *Flinging the billows back from my drench'd hair,*
> *And laughing from my lip the audacious brine. ...*

This has the 'shallowness' of classical Greek poetry, and reminds one in particular of the boasting at the Phaeacian games in *The Odyssey*. There is no more of the complex verbal icon in Homer or Pindar than there is in Byron. The Greeks, the Romans, Chaucer, Pope and Cowper are worlds away from the Elizabethans, Donne, Shelley and Wordsworth. Imagery in the style of the paradox or crossword-puzzle is rare in Byron; his paradoxes are obvious and meant as fun; his puzzles exist in his themes only. Certainly, much of what he wrote was intended to be the object of prolonged meditation, but not of prolonged mining for meaning. Odd as it may seem, he is one of the least idiosyncratic writers in English. Discard the exotic

content of his poetry, and you have someone much closer to
Chaucer than to Shelley. It is his personal problems which
bring him into mind with Baudelaire; his main stylistic concern
is to keep his vision clear. He can be as direct as Chaucer:

> *Perceiving that the pig was on him close,*
> *He gave him such a punch upon the head,*
> *As floor'd him so that he no more arose,*
> *Smashing the very bone; and he fell dead*
> *Next to the other.*

as physical as Gide is in *Fruits of the Earth*:

> *The mat for rest; for dress the fresh gnatoo,*
> *And sandal oil to fence against the dew;*
> *For food the cocoa-nut, the yam, the bread*
> *Born of the fruit; for board the plantain spread*
> *With its broad leaf. . . .*

as organized in motion as Milton:

> *I do not combat against death, but thee*
> *And thy surrounding angels; my past power,*
> *Was purchased by no compact with thy crew,*
> *But by superior science – penance, daring,*
> *And length of watching, strength of mind, and skill*
> *In knowledge of our fathers –*

as chiming as Verlaine:

> *The city lies sleeping;*
> *The morn to deplore it,*
> *May dawn on it weeping :*
> *Sullenly, slowly,*
> *The black plague flew o'er it –*

76

as terse as Landor:

> *If solitude succeed to grief,*
> *Release from pain is slight relief;*
> *The vacant bosom's wilderness*
> *Might thank the pang that made it less.*
> *We loathe what none are left to share....*

As alert to borrow from Shakespeare as Mr Eliot – 'cold Obstruction's apathy'[1]; and as graphic as Blake or Villon:

> *Here Folly still his votaries inthrals;*
> *And young-eyed Lewdness walks her midnight rounds;*
> *Girt with the silent crimes of Capitals....*

He is adept in fitting talk into his couplets:

INK.: *Then at two hours past midnight we all meet again,*
For the sciences, sandwiches, hock, and champagne!
TRA.: *And the sweet lobster salad!*
BOTH.: *I honour that meal;*
For 'tis then that our feelings most genuinely – feel.
INK.: *True; feeling is truest then, far beyond question:*
I wish to the gods 'twas the same with digestion!

He redisposes the stresses by breaking up the line:

> *'A strange sail in the offing.' – 'Sail! and how?*
> *What! could you make her out? It cannot be....'*

He has a full command of the epic formula, which calls for non-symbolic images. He never puts obscure words in simple phrasing, but some of his simplicities are tortuously unwound. He is the master of half-rhyme:

> *Beside the jutting rock the few appear'd,*
> *Like the last remnant of the red-deer's herd....*

---

[1] And as open about it: a note to *The Giaour* refers us to ' "To lie in cold obstruction?" (*Measure for Measure*, Act iii. Sc. 1).'

And most of all, he serves to remind us that great poetry need not be metaphorical in the least:

> *Though the night was made for loving,*
> *And the day returns too soon,*
> *Yet we'll go no more a roving*
> *By the light of the moon.*

The pathetic, constricting effect of that last line is an object-lesson in use of context; and he was supreme in the arrangement of contrast. He is all enamels, cameos and talk; but he is also capable of whipping out a line that has a scrubbed look:

MAN.: *What is the hour?*
HER: *It wants but one till sunset,*
And promises a lovely twilight.

That line has all the cosiness of Hemingway's secular raptures; and it looks lame, unspecial on the page. Yet it is more essentially dramatic than his fulsome invocations to the 'Glorious Orb'.

Obviously, nearly everything in Byron's poetry, whether exotic or farcical, is larger than life. The morality is concerned with clean-cut issues – with evil not lesser evils, and the action with prevailing or going under – not comparative failure, but the utter miscarriage of everything. So it is not surprising that he settled into fustian, and set out to write poetry without much authentic stimulus. Animation degenerates into device. Time and again he leaps onto the rhyming horse, rides for long stretches, but merely expends energy. Even his worst is various, though: as various as his best. He often wrote carelessly, but with ingenious disregard.

As a survey of his imagery shows, he had a vast collection of items he could draw upon. But rarely are his permutations striking. He lacks the audacious vision that enabled Baudelaire to use shoddy paraphernalia without loss of intensity. To a large extent, the magic of words – the sudden emancipation from cliché – is concealed from him; ironically so, for if anyone resented ordinariness or suetude, it was Byron. He cannot fuse dissimilar items except by resorting to the stock conjunctions; but he can exploit novel dissimilarities to the point of idiocy; and that is his gift:

> My dear Mr Murray,
> You're in a damn'd hurry,
>   To set up this ultimate Canto;
> But (if they don't rob us)
> You'll see Mr Hobhouse
> Will bring it safe in his portmanteau.

An earlier piece, 'The Devil's Drive' – quaintly sub-titled 'An Unfinished Rhapsody' – is in the same vein:

> The Devil return'd to hell by two,
>   And he stay'd at home till five;
> When he dined on some homicides done in ragoût,
>   And a rebel or so in an Irish stew,
>   And sausages made of a self-slain Jew. . . .

Perhaps the only poems in which he is both evidently and deeply sincere are those about the separation from his wife. There is spleen, attitudinizing, high-flown righteousness and a startled heart in these poems: Byron, incongruously earnest, is faintly ridiculous, which he never is in the poems to Augusta. Here is an excerpt from the 'Lines On Hearing That Lady Byron Was Ill', written in 1816:

> . . . the mind recoils
> Upon itself, and the wreck'd heart lies cold,
> While heaviness collects the shatter'd spoils.
> It is not in the storm nor in the strife
> We feel benumb'd, and wish to be no more,
> But in the after-silence on the shore,
> When all is lost, except a little life.

Very subdued, it is the product of his need to eliminate; but he suppresses what his style cannot carry. Phrases like 'the moral Clytemnestra of thy lord' are hysterically earnest, and betray what he might have written if he had not poured much of the darkest stuff into his letters. Some of the calmer phrasing, however, is lapidary and deadly:

> . . . *the significant eye*
> *Which learns to lie with silence – the pretext*
> *Of prudence, with advantages annex'd –*
> *The acquiescence in all things which tend,*
> *No matter how, to the desired end –*
> *All found a place in thy philosophy.*

It might be an apostrophe on any lickspittle; he has the range of his target now. There is in all of his acutely personal poems a clouding perception, together with a decline in technical proficiency: he lives up to the demands of his art only when he is attacking, being impersonal and depreciating by farce. He never did get Lady Byron into focus in terms of anguish and humiliation; in terms of animus, yes. And the various pieces to Augusta constantly verge on the maudlin.

As I have said, he kept narrowing his definition of the poetic; and the shelved private topics he could not manage kept troubling him. A various poet, he was not adaptable, although his 'Occasional Pieces' include some virile satire and some serene, vague lyrics of a type he used in the plays:

> *But the hound bayeth loudly,*
> *The boar's in the wood,*
> *And the falcon longs proudly*
> *To spring from her hood :*
> *On the wrist of the noble*
> *She sits like a crest,*
> *And the air is in trouble*
> *With birds from their nest.*

THE FARCE WITH LANGUAGE

That is from *The Deformed Transformed* – not very different from *Stanzas*:

> Could Love for ever
> Run like a river,
> And Time's endeavour
>   Be tried in vain –
> No other pleasure
> With this could measure;
> And like a treasure
> We'd hug the chain.

These little incantations rise straight and clear from familiar situations: there is little attempt to transform the situations – by tight manœuvering with bold images or by sheer sound – into something magical. But the rest of the occasional pieces are rather tedious: damp epigrams, leaden Odes, Versicles, the febrile 'Darkness', the fulsome anthem 'The Irish Avatar'. None of them approaches those few perfectly realized and almost impersonal lyrics, 'There be none of Beauty's daughters', 'She walks in beauty . . .', or even, for gusto, the galumphing 'Stanzas Written On The Road Between Florence and Pisa':

> Oh, talk not to me of a name great in story;
> The days of our youth are the days of our glory. . . .

Less than three years after writing those stanzas he was dead, with the poetry of marital and sexual anguish still inside him, and only awkwardly hinted at elsewhere.

What is it, then, that stales his infinite variety, keeps him unread in England and canonized abroad? The life as pageant and legend is partly to blame. So too is the subject-matter of island idyll, Levantine intrigue, dagger-and-cloak stuff from Italian history, vast *Weltschmerz,* the quasi-Biblical, squabbles of literary and social sects, 'frozen mummies on the Polar

plains,' forgotten Pharoahs, Caesars, Kosciusko. . . . This is
the matter of the film world; and one day an enterprising pro-
ducer will set about Byron as others have set about Emily
Brontë, Robert Louis Stevenson, P. C. Wren, Rider Haggard,
Scott and, of course, Mary Shelley. And then there will be an
even better excuse for leaving him unread. The best is attain-
able only through reading; and that, of course, is *Don Juan,
The Vision, Beppo* and some of *Childe Harold*. As it is, he remains
a great comic poet, a blend of Jonson and La Rochefoucauld;
and, for the rest, as minor in his pulp as Southey and Rogers.
The reasons for both seem implicit in his approving quotation
of the following story:

Sir W. D. was a great gamester. Coming in one day to the club of
which he was a member, he was observed to look melancholy.
'What is the matter, Sir William?' cried Hare, of facetious memory.
'Ah!' replied Sir W., 'I have just lost poor Lady D.' – '*Lost*! What
at? *Quinze* or *Hazard*?' was the consolatory rejoinder of the querist.

A great gamester, of facetious memory? He was all of that, and
rich in the consolatory rejoinders too. His game had one serious
purpose; he told Murray that '*Don Juan* will be known by and
by, for what it is intended, – a *Satire* on *abuses* of the present
states of Society'. It was derision, not homily; confirmatory
rather than remedial. Three years earlier (26th October 1819)
he had written to Douglas Kinnaird that *Don Juan* 'is the sublime of *that there* sort of writing – it may be bawdy but is it not
good English? It may be profligate but is it not *life,* is it not
the thing?' It was all four. It lacked only what Sir Herbert
Grierson called 'a deeper pity for the human heart that suffers
and is defeated in this strange, meaningless pageant'. The lack,
I think, is the result of Byron's self-consciousness; there is no
question of an inability to feel. He felt; perhaps too much. In
his actual living he experienced, as Charles du Bos said, a
besoin de la fatalité – a need to feel that he was *meant* to do this or

that. But the feeling of inevitability that he eventually gained when he set sail for Greece on 13th July 1823 was denied him in his writing life. For Byron the writer, it all came to this: 'if I don't write to empty my mind, I go mad . . . [yet] I think composition a great pain'. His writing is compulsive; but is it destined? Writing is a pain: it makes him self-conscious. He is torn between madness and pain; he vacillates between wanting to write and wanting not to. The clear decisions of the heroic life are not here; all is clouded with psychology.

So it was much easier to write casually. He had not so much to choose the right words as to let words come. They came; but he had enough sense not to regard the spontaneous overflow as perfect. He was only too conscious of the arbitrary nature of his release-writing. But he could not, he said, bear to work on his lines, to make them deeper. And his abdication from the deeper pity, from the final and purposeful language it entails, ensures his pre-eminence in comedy although also his negative pose.

Chapter 4

THE ROMANCES

Campbell is lecturing, Moore idling, Southey twaddling, Wordsworth driveling, Coleridge muddling, Joanna Baillie piddling, Bowles quibbling, squabbling and snivelling. . . . The pity . . . is, that they never lived either in *high life*, nor in *solitude*. . . .

(*Letters and Journals*, V, 362-3)

BYRON wrote his verse romances easily and often negligently. In some the versification is rough, and the rattle of the lines is not that consequent on a scrupulous avoidance of monotony. But there are, here and there, modulated and immediate passages over which he seems to have spent some time or which felicitously explore a *trouvaille*. Yet, good or bad, the versification has to be noticed only in passing; for if you are to read these romances – especially the most contrived ones like *The Giaour* and *The Bride of Abydos* – you have to read at some speed. There are too many digressions: the interpretation of incident and the scrutiny of attitude constantly distract Byron from getting on with the story. If you read quickly, the rhythm or at least the agitation of life makes itself felt. If you linger with the poet in his contemplative digressions, you come nearer the man, certainly, but lose the current of action.

This should not be so; an attentiveness to commentary should not enfeeble our sense of the narrative. But Byron was an involuntary writer, and failed to distinguish between composing speed and reading speed. When he wrote he had only composing speed in mind. Most writers, of course, try to allow for this time-lag: what is laboriously devised may not cause the reading eye itself to labour, but to skid. The easily written may delay the reader. But Byron, looking too closely, inquiring too curiously, tended to lose perspective. That is, he knew where he was, and why, and where the story went next; but he could not imagine how all this would look to the reader. And, as narrative poems go, those of Byron never really get going like those of Chaucer, Keats and Tennyson. His couplet stays too far from the spoken language and becomes recitative – a sounding declamation. His trucks seem too wide for his rails. He does not infuse enough pace into the action for the establishment of tension during the reflective parts. In consequence, the story seems not so much forced off course as severed. When we accompany the narrative poet into a digression, we should feel a sense of strain; we should feel that the story is being dammed up, and that its impetus is not to be governed for long. But the narratives of Byron are (to resume an earlier metaphor) trucks coupled together. Or rather, we are often shown couplings which are never used. The ghost of Childe Harold keeps slowing things up.

It would be idle to pretend that Byron's verse romances are likely to win multitudes of readers. His dramatic poems might, for they at least give us talk, life's exchanges, and expose the source of action. But the romances lack even the amplitude in meditation, the exhibitory skill, of *Childe Harold*. Of course, *The Island* and *The Corsair* are more readable than the others: there is a greater variety of imagery; the origins and issues are not deliberately obfuscated, and there is almost enough action to balance the brooding. But even these two poems lose likeness to life for a present-day taste that has been either brainwashed or repelled by Hollywood. Byron, we might say, was writing for brains comparatively unwashed. But he was doing more: he was fusing the exotic with self-conscious confession. And his themes in these romances give an added insight into the attitudes adopted in the narrative and manner of *Don Juan*.

There is no point in trying to isolate and define too closely these themes, for Byron himself failed to distinguish between exile and mere loneliness, between illicit and incestuous love, between self-obsession and gaol, between even heartbreak and death. These are the themes, certainly, but in turning to them quite naturally, Byron used them loosely, He separated them from any direct bearing on his own life, but at the same time assembled them into a negligent conspectus of his own personality. The relationships between illicit love and exile, between exile and the sense of guilt, between aloofness and callousness, are not fully worked out.

exilos

All we need to know is that Lara, Manfred, Conrad, the Giaour, Alp, Christian and the Childe are exiles, for one reason or another: crime, hubris, demonic possession, illegality of love or piracy, intrigue, mutiny, scandal. And they are exiled against their will. They constitute the weird charade into which Byron poured so much of the self he had to eliminate. Much of his work is concerned with conscience in alienation, with the trapped man and his longing for exculpation. When Byron was writing, none of this was very new. Byron refers only once to Chateaubriand, in that strange round-the-world-in-778-lines poem, *The Age of Bronze*, but he does acknowledge one debt in the preface of *Werner*:

When I was young (about fourteen, I think), I first read this tale, which made a deep impression upon me; and may, indeed, be said to contain the germ of much that I have since written.

Certainly the 'inherent weakness, half-humanity, selfish remorse, and temporizing pity' mentioned at the end of *Werner* seem to come under the stricture passed in *René* by Father Souel: 'One is not a superior being merely because one sees this world in an odious light.' He goes on to say of René, 'Presumptuous young man, he imagines that any individual is sufficient unto himself! Solitude is an evil thing for any creature who does not live in God.' The interesting thing is that in his narrative poems, Byron makes so many allusions to Christianity. A constant theme is hubris expiated; but this high drama on the frontiers of salvation seems to be presented for the wrong reasons: it is intensely exotic; utopia, fortunately, means 'nowhere'. Take Lara, for instance:

> *There was in him a vital scorn of all :*
> *As if the worst had fall'n which could befall,*
> *He stood a stranger in this breathing world,*
> *An erring spirit from another hurl'd;*
> *A thing of dark imaginings, that shaped*
> *By choice the perils he by chance escaped. . . .*

That looks clear enough. Lara liked his pose; Byron liked presenting it. Lara was an extremist and an addict of the absolute. He wounded Otho in combat, but not seriously:

> *Yet look'd he on him still with eye intent,*
> *As if he loathed the ineffectual strife*
> *That left a foe, howe'er o'ercome, with life. . . .*

Here, I believe, is one of the important influences upon Byron's literary practice. He had to seek an absolute or to make fun of everything; to be serious was to be extremist, to be anything else entailed heartless farce. He had the choice between over-response or none. Some trick of temperament began it; some vicissitudes in his social leap accentuated it, and perhaps a reading of *René* in his teens made it worse. At any rate, he had only two ways.

When he was serious, Heaven was exotic; when he was farcing, it was the supreme butt. When he was serious, he wrote of extreme predicaments; when he was not, he found no predicament extreme enough to warrant sympathy. He had to switch between the dying Lara who rejects the crucifix and the more arrant rejection of *The Vision of Judgment*. It is strange how many women in his poems die of heartbreak. Kaled in *Lara*, Zuleika in *The Bride of Abydos*, Medora in *The Corsair*, Francesca in *The Siege of Corinth* and possibly, the poet suggests,

Parisina, all exchange this world for the next with minimum fuss. Such transits suggest lack of compromise as a theme. It did not perturb Byron to hold contradictory views; but he could not bear to exchange the two for a compromise between them. (One is reminded of Scott Fitzgerald's idea that the mark of an intelligent man is the ability to hold opposed views simultaneously without losing power of responsible action.) In a similar way, Hemingway's characters are always hovering between anguish and apathy. The middle way is the penurious one: it is always easier to think in terms of Hell and Heaven, Good and Evil, Body and Soul, Death and Life, than it is to tack sensitively between them in the course of one's life.

Consider the trapped men of Byron's narratives. The Giaour loves, avenges and dies, all without moderation. The outline of his action is clear, and there is little in his career save extreme acts and intense states of mind. Selim, in *The Bride of Abydos*, might have wasted time vacillating between caution and loathing. But when the poem begins, he has to save Zuleika from an arranged marriage and is committed to a series of justified acts. Byron picks his men when they have gone beyond half-attitudes. Conrad the pirate has to ambush, has to escape, has to vanish for good on the death of Medora. Hugo, in love with his stepmother Parisina, has alternatives of madness or the axe. Alp and Christian have to do something extreme: one turns traitor; the other mutinies and turns outlaw. Even the Prisoner of Chillon 'learn'd to love despair':

> *It was at length the same to me,*
> *Fetter'd or fetterless to be. . . .*
>
> .   .   .   .   .
>
> *And thus when they appear'd at last,*
> *And all my bonds aside were cast,*
> *These heavy walls to me had grown*
> *A hermitage – and all my own!*

Despair is an extreme attitude – one that has had a remarkable career as a literary pose, and one that brings Byron into the company of Hemingway, Cesare Pavese the eventual suicide, and Ernst Jünger with his cult of 'the deathly realm'. The Byronic sources – Voltaire's *Charles XII*, Turkish legend and history, Gibbon, Bligh's account of the *Bounty* mutiny, Goethe – are varied and, for the most part, exotic. They give Byron a start in the race to objectify; they put the subject far from home and make it more of a 'thing'. Hemingway relates all to nature, to his own special idea of Mark Twain's 'Territory', but not to responsible individuality. Pavese, before his suicide, consigned his perilous matter to his Journal, and Jünger made the juggernaut of war his absolute. With all four, the traffic between the life and the art is out of control: the art recommends and fulfils what in life is impossible. If these men had not encountered the impossible, they would not have started writing. They share the assumption that man can achieve a salvation and a reconciliation without reference to the world at all. This frightful burden on personal identity annihilates most of Byron's protagonists. Those who survive – Mazeppa the dedicated Polish warrior, The Prisoner of Chillon, half-way to apathy – seem to have no idea of where they are going. The implication is that they have not enough sense of sin to need a reconciliation. Bonnivard the prisoner stops short of revenge; so does Mazeppa – the man of action, although both have grievance enough. Resentment is not guilt or revenge, and the moral identity of each man is intact. They feel nothing of the chorus of execration in that dreary apocalyptic pageant, *Heaven and Earth*:

> *We deem our curses vain; we must expire;*
> *But as we know the worst,*
> *Why should our hymn be raised, our knees be bent*
> *Before the implacable Omnipotent,*
> *Since we must fall the same?*

> *If he hath made earth, let it be his shame,*
> *To make a world for torture.*

There is a pervasive idea in Byron's writings that God regards men as *objects* but failed to create them as such. In consequence, men are compelled into callous attitudes in order to protect their spirits, and even seek to redefine themselves without God. But such a pursuit is vain – as the First Destiny in *Manfred* points out:

> *. . . knowledge is not happiness, and science*
> *But an exchange of ignorance for that*
> *Which is another kind of ignorance.*

And Manfred, for all his acquired wisdom, can neither pre-empt his after-life nor evade it. The mind may be its own ministrant but, as Father Souel says in *René*, cannot be an absolute. The following is therefore an heroic but futile assertion:

> *The mind which is immortal makes itself*
> *Requital for its good or evil thoughts, –*
> *Is its own origin of ill and end –*
> *And its own place and time: its innate sense,*
> *When stripp'd of this mortality, derives*
> *No colour from the fleeting things without,*
> *But is absorb'd in sufferance or in joy,*
> *Born from the knowledge of its own desert.*

But just because there can be a mental hell and heaven, that does not mean that the mind controls either. The trouble is that the urge to establish and preserve a moral identity often brings solipsism. Nearly all Byron's heroes have had predica-ments forced upon them; and they seek, by working for evil or good, to regain control of themselves and of their own destiny. They cannot forestall the imposition upon them of rôles; but they can seek emancipation. Byron chooses constantly an unnerving sense of one's own malleable identity rather than a despairing submission to fraud. That was why be behaved coquettishly about his last mission: he was defining himself by accepting his election to the Greek Committee, and all that the acceptance entailed. (One wonders why M. Sartre has not fixed his attention on Byron's whims for simultaneous *disponibilité* and commitment.) The Byron who died at rain-soaked Missolonghi had not expected to survive. He vacillated a good deal before he left for Greece; but, once committed and on his way, he began to interpret his actions in terms of 'destiny'. His vacillations were meant to convince himself that he was unattached – to Teresa Guiccioli or to the Greek cause. His increasing sense of destiny forestalled any waning of purpose. In fact he forced his death upon himself in much the same way as he forced himself into 'poor Greece'.

Consider for a moment those outsiders, the Byronic *hommes traqués*. Childe Harold dissolves into a Baedeker – 'I live not in myself, but I become Portion of that around me'; he is anxious to efface and eliminate. This is an elementary stage: what he brought upon himself he has to shed. Beyond that he has no need to go, for no one opposes him. But the Giaour, a Christian, feels obliged to avenge the woman he stole. He does kill her murderer, but dies of remorse. In *The Bride of Abydos*, Selim is being passed off as Giaffir's son, whereas he is really the son of Giaffir's brother, whom Giaffir murdered. But when Selim tries to escape with Zuleika, Giaffir murders him too. Conrad the Corsair, 'too firm to yield, and far too proud to stoop', is doomed from the start. Forced into piracy, he finds that only his love for Medora keeps life worth living. When she dies, he can neither seek another life nor survive. Lara, always aloof, leads the serfs against Otho – though with some reluctance. But there is no escape: he is killed, as is Alp the exiled Venetian who has to lead a Tartar attack on Corinth. And Hugo, finding himself in an intolerable position – lover of the woman (Parisina) who is compelled to become his stepmother – is beheaded. Cain is of the devil's party to start with. Not one of these characters rebels without working his own dissolution. The poetry is in the impossibility of their predicaments. Doom is the price of their singularity – or *are* they singular at all? If there is any point in these fatalistic fables, is it one that bears on living? Or are they merely operatic?

Of course, on one level of interpretation, Byron's verse romances illustrate perfectly the world of Albert Camus – absurd with or without God. And from such a perception of doom as Byron has, it would be no difficult matter to deduce an absolute of hopelessness. The characters are not tested, they are eliminated. Life closes in, and the odds are impossible. Before he goes under, the protagonist may discover some part of the truth: the Giaour the force of his creed; Selim his own courage; Conrad the lie he has been living; Lara the sense of his own gifts as a demagogue; Alp the irrevocableness of his disguise; Hugo the arbitrary nature of law. These men are very much alone in their false rôles and unusual predicaments. For a short while, some of them bridge the gulf. The Giaour confesses; Selim comes into an even deeper affinity with Zuleika; Conrad encounters another woman, Gulnare, one who will murder for him; Lara manages to identify himself with the popular cause; Alp finds Francesca again; Hugo expresses himself fully to his father:

> Begot in sin, to die in shame,
> My life begun and ends the same :
> As err'd the sire, so err'd the son,
> And thou must punish both in one.
> My crime seems worst to human view,
> But God must judge between us too!

This is the oldest mode of tragedy: an accepted condition has been repudiated, the hero suddenly discovers a newly hostile world with which he has to come to terms. Byron's array of estranged souls is similar to that of Joseph Conrad, although some of Byron's situations are a little more *recherché* and illustrious. Compare the Corsair with Heyst in *Victory*. This is the Corsair:

> *He knew himself detested, but he knew*
> *The hearts that loath'd him, crouch'd and dreaded too.*
> *Lone, wild, and strange, he stood alike exempt*
> *From all affection and from all contempt. . . .*

This is Heyst:

Heyst was not conscious of either friends or enemies. It was the very essence of his life to be a solitary achievement, accomplished not by hermit-like withdrawal with its silence and immobility, but by a system of restless wandering, by the detachment of an impermanent dweller amongst changing scenes. In this scheme he had perceived the means of passing through life without suffering and almost without a care in the world – invulnerable because elusive.

But there was a soft spot in the Corsair:

> *None are all evil – quickening round his heart*
> *One softer feeling would not yet depart;*
> *Oft could he sneer at others as beguiled*
> *By passions worthy of a fool or child;*
> *Yet 'gainst that passion vainly still he strove,*
> *And even in him it asks the name of Love!*

And this love for Medora both nurtured and undid him. Heyst too had a vulnerable point: he could never belittle a 'decent feeling'; that fact both undermines him and brings him through. But Byron, in his verse romances at least, gives only spasmodically that movement of conscience so prominent in Conrad.

Byron, we must not forget, was providing entertainments adapted, rather like those of Graham Greene, to the temper of the age, but also to his own requirements and preferences. And he made little effort to discipline his preferences: that is to say, he gives many passages which appear to exert the same pressure on us as the tragic chorus, but confer none of that device's illumination, none of its healing. Although Byron describes the mental motions of his characters, he constantly subjects them to the presence of mystery. He is always hinting at some frightful secret, some gross blunder. His heroes are either permutations of Cain or men who have been plotted against. The consequence is that they evoke a stereotype and start from melodrama. There is a world of difference between an intensely dramatic situation and one that seems intensified by allusion to a general pattern. The first type of situation always looks – in terms of art, that is – immediate; the second, at one remove. The first (say *An Outcast of the Islands*, a Conrad fiction) is much less melodramatic than Byron's version of the *Bounty* story in *The Island*. The Conrad is exotic and preposterous, but is so because it contains many elements of the unfamiliar. The Byron is exotic only in so far as it survives the preposterous typing to which Byron subjects his characters:

> *For me, my lot is what I sought; to be,*
> *In life or death, the fearless and the free.*

Conrad's handling of a fiction compels us to suspend incredulity; Byron's version of the true suspends credulity. The trouble is that Byron fails to control the tone: the supervising mind that swiftly relates the narrative to familiar melodrama betrays itself in frivolities, or near-frivolities, that foreshadow *Don Juan*. Byron has begun to explore the topsy-turvy farce that can be extracted from the language:

> *Jack was embarrass'd, – never hero more,*
> *And as he knew not what to say, he swore:*

94

> *Nor swore in vain; the long congenial sound*
> *Revived Ben Bunting from his pipe profound;*
> *He drew it from his mouth, and look'd full wise,*
> *But merely added to the oath his eyes;*
> *Thus rendering the imperfect phrase complete,*
> *A peroration I need not repeat.*

Melodrama is self-conscious; and Byron's self-consciousness in this poem is destructive, quite vitiating Christian's resolve to evacuate the natives and to fight things out. The point is that Byron cannot have it both ways. A theme not seriously presented cannot be included in a congeries of similar but seriously presented themes. In short, Byron has to express or travesty. In *The Island* his attention is as much to the language as to ethics:

> *These, with a bayonet, not so free from rust*
> *As when the arm-chest held its brighter trust,*
> *Completed his accoutrements, as Night*
> *Surveyed him in his garb heteroclite.*

That last word is quite gratuitous, and does some exquisite wrecking. It evinces the Byronic instability. After all, if a man cannot take himself seriously, he is hardly likely to present seriously those themes that might seem to implicate his own life.

The Byronic characters would have a spendid reason to do a Pirandello on their author. He is more concerned with displaying his temperament than with resolving any putative problems of his own. The temperament permits anything in the art, and Byron usually ends up as puppeteer. The poetry is in the incongruity. To add flippancy to melodrama is to produce farce of an unnerving kind; for the flippancy *may* be the despairing gesture of a serious sensibility. The Dadaists were melodramatic and flippant, but for the purpose of expressing disgust with a civilization which had let them down. Sometimes only the hysterical, the manic, the crass, affords a satisfactory means of self-expression. In Byron the *grand guignol* and the farcical assist the expression of a tragic mood; only the deliberately abortive has any power to restore.

What, then, of the characters whose agonies take up so many lines? Are they not merely figments, but plaster absurdities like Christian Morgenstern's Herr von Korf, Palmström and the Nasobem? Do they belong in the world of the following?

Palmström constructs an olfactory organ and plays von Korf's sneezewort sonata on it.

It begins with triplets of alpine herbs and produces an enchanting effect with an acacia-blossom aria.

But in the scherzo, sudden and unexpected, between tuberoses and eucalyptus, there ensue the three famous sneezewort passages, from which the sonata takes its name.

Byron's escapades with feminine rhyme have the same twisting of the conventional as this; but he was never delicate-handed to the same extent. His touch was more robust, although it could achieve the firm gentleness of the idylls in *The Island*. Everything, in fact, is robust except his guiding hand to the reader. We are left to answer questions not merely academic and of our own invention, but those important to us if we make the attempt to read him entire. One question is especially important: if we are in doubt as to his intention, must we read according to his temperament, and assume that he intends to be farcical? I think this would be unwise. True, Byron was an inconsistent person, and in his best work made an aesthetic out of irresponsibility. But to devise for him a fixed literary self is to ask for trouble. It would be to assume that he had no control over his contrasts: an absurd assumption. He has, in fact, three main selves, and on occasion makes fun of them all.

First there is the exoticist of the romances; second the polemical author on literary and social themes; and third the intrusive, self-conscious creator. We have a projection, a poet

in person, and a very personal impresario; and *Don Juan* is a
mixture of all three. Of these, the last is the dominant. The
person is too big for the poet, just as the biography has been
too much for the poetry. The 'polemical working' and restless
quality that Arnold complained about were the very signs of
sincerity. We are apt, I think, to identify the sincere with the
homogeneous: a complex attitude that is sincere is a constant
in few minds. There is a general and unenlightened assumption
that Edna Millay and Keats, to take usual examples, are more
sincere than, say, La Rochefoucauld and Wallace Stevens.
Unmixed feelings, unironic attitudes, seem in some people's
minds to exhaust the sincere – and this in spite of Mr Eliot's
efforts to rehabilitate the mixed moods of Donne, Marvell and
Johnson. All this, of course, is very bad for the Byrons. Look
at the Byronic make-up: no philosopher, he prefers attitudes
and moods; highly self-conscious, ashamed of *Hours of Idleness*,
he wants to be popular and yet sincere.

Surely he co-ordinated all this as well as anyone could have
done. While he was writing his greatest poem, sincerity in the
form of acute self-consciousness took over; and he guys the rôle
of impresario only to keep us on the ground: after all, he seems
to point out, this is only a poem, you know! What irritates
many who have taken the trouble to read Byron entire is his
unelevated view of his art. His writing – the act, the long nights,
the search for a stanza-form – were all near enough to the
Schadenfreude of his life to preclude absolute poses. His sincerity
was that of shyness. *Don Juan* is not only sincere; it is serious,
which is to say that the poem is undertaken deliberately and
with full accommodation of the means to a clear end. This is
more than we can say for *Prometheus Unbound, The Prelude* and
Hyperion. Byron's poem is the richest in knowledge of experience, however disclaimed, and eloquent in every stanza of the
inadequacy he had found among the simple colours of romance.
The Island marks the change from simple to complex, from

deliberate solemnity to deliberate half-seriousness. Humour
disturbs this poem; but the humour is an integer, not a manner-
ism. Not this, from the nose-thumbing poem on Elgin, *The
Curse of Minerva*:

> *Daughter of Jove! in Britain's injured name,*
> *A true-born Briton may the deed disclaim.*
> *Frown not on England ; England owns him not:*
> *Athena, no! thy plunderer was a Scot.*

but this kind of thing, deft and complicating:

> *His cutlass droop'd, unconscious of a sheath,*
> *Or lost or worn away; his pistols were*
> *Link'd to his belt, a matrimonial pair –*
> *(Let not this metaphor appear a scoff,*
> *Though one miss'd fire, the other would go off. . . .)*

But when Byron tired of the simplified, he turned not only to
humour but also to the serious and complex verse play. And
where we might fault his romances with shallowness, his
comedy with complexity, we find in the dramas a patient
exploration of substantial themes. The give and take of personal
intercourse enables Byron to study feeling from many points
of view, to anatomize more fully passion and its reciprocity,
to exchange digression for soliloquy – even to demonstrate the
futility of any kind of understanding. These plays, none of
them intended for the stage, and accommodated to Byron's
idea of the unities, were written while Byron was finishing
Don Juan. They comprise the feelings and situations which in
Don Juan were summed up with sophisticated, knowing famili-
arity. They might thus be said to constitute the overflow or the
matériel of the long poem – the clinical research behind the
brilliant report. But several cantos of *Don Juan* had been completed before *Marino Faliero, The Two Foscari, Sardanapalus,
Cain* and *Heaven and Earth* were even begun. The image comes

to mind of the gifted anticipator who produces an off-the-cuff masterpiece (or at least a third of it) and quickly devises workbooks in case the examiners want to look. But overspill, compensation, private empiricism – whatever they are, the plays are of great interest, for they show Byron in an unusual aspect: without wit, without rhyme, but almost desperately philosophical.

Chapter 5

THE PLAYS

> . . . my dramatic simplicity is *studiously* Greek, and must continue
> so: *no* reform ever succeeded at first. I admire the old English
> dramatists; but this is quite another field, and has nothing to do with
> theirs. I want to make a *regular* English drama, no matter whether
> for the Stage or not, which is not my object, – but a *mental*
> *theatre.*
> (Letter to Murray, 23rd August 1821)

> The Simplicity of the plot is intentional, and the avoidance of
> *rant* also, as also the compression of the Speeches in the more
> severe situations.
> (Letter to Murray, 20th September 1821)

RANGING from the turgid 'mystery' pastiche *Heaven and Earth*
to the surrealistic farrago *The Deformed Transformed*, Byron's
plays present in a more animated manner than the romances
the theme of the trapped man. The action takes place very
much under the aspect (and almost beneath the dignity) of
eternity; and tends to surfeit the mind's eye, at which it is
aimed. The nature of the theme itself has an effect of depopu-
lating the plays; and, oddly enough, the surrealism of *The
Deformed Transformed* has more flavour of everyday life than
the others have. These plays are pageants *à thèse*, at once explor-
ing further the theme of the romances and falling short of the
philosophical interpretations they promise. Byron, as ever, is
more interested in emotions than in ideas, in attitudes rather
than motives, in flourish rather than steady observation, in
similitudes rather than analysis.

The situations, on their respective levels, are similar. Marino
Faliero, Doge of Venice, has more dignity than power: Michel
Steno has carelessly smirched the reputation of the Doge's
wife; but the Forty, the omnipotent synod of which Steno is
a member, merely order a token punishment of a month's

close arrest. Feeling that he counts for nothing, that he, his office, family and forbears have been insulted, the Doge joins and leads an insurrection which fails. He is tried, sentenced and beheaded within the hour.

Sardanapalus, effete and despised king of Nineveh and Assyria, is renowned for a clemency that has in it more of indolence than high principle. His life is one long, languid debauch: surrounded by concubines and wearing a crown of flowers, he preaches pacifism while the forces of treason slowly gather. He lives apart from his queen and children, and spends most of his time with Myrrha, an Ionian female slave. Only Salemenes, his brother-in-law, can see what the outcome will be. He tries to convince the king; but Sardanapalus only half-attends until, in fact, a *coup d'état* is almost complete, and the insurgents are within his palace. Then the transformation occurs: sybarite becomes warrior, inspired and indefatigable – but in vain. So, after giving away his treasure to the survivors, evacuating his wife and children with the rest, he and Myrrha set fire to the palace, and burn together. He thus preserves the line of Nimrod although the rebels prevail.

In *The Two Foscari*, the Doge's son is being tried for plotting against the state. Many think this a trumped-up charge, and that the real motive of certain members of the Council of Ten is the extermination of the Foscari line. No sooner has the son been sentenced to exile than he dies from the effect of accumulated torture. The Doge is then asked to resign, and eventually agrees. Preparing to leave the ducal palace in state, he calls for water, takes a poisoned cup from Loredano, the most vindictive of the plotters, and dies instantly.

In *Werner*, its seriousness broken by the egregious and Falstaffian Gabor, Werner seeks in his own honourable way the inheritance from which he has been barred. But his son Ulric murders Stralenheim, who stands in their way, and discloses this fact to his father only as the play ends, with Werner

CARL A. RUDISILL LIBRARY
LENOIR RHYNE COLLEGE

become Count Siegendorf. Byron's interpretation of this is in terms of the trapped man; these two trap each other: 'a son pre-destined to evil by the weakness and sensuality of his father, a father punished for his want of rectitude by the passionate criminality of his son'. Byron first read the original tale (in Lee's *Canterbury Tales*) when he was about fourteen. It made a deep impression on him; and in the Preface he says that it 'may, indeed, be said to contain the germ of much that I have since written'. It may: there is an Old Testament grimness in much of his work. But, in his view, vengeance and retribution come in *this* life; indeed, in the Preface to *Cain*, he asks the reader 'to bear in mind (what few choose to recollect), that there is no allusion to a future state in any of the books of Moses, nor indeed in the Old Testament.'

Of the plays that resort to the supernatural, *The Deformed Transformed* sees Arnold the hunchback magically transformed into the shape of Achilles, and joining in an attack on Rome; *Manfred* enacts the pursuit of oblivion, power and immortality; *Cain* shows the apostate becoming the criminal; and *Heaven and Earth* illustrates the folly of brooking divine decree. The themes are typical of Byron's half-pagan eschatology; and they are not always clearly presented. It almost seems as if the attempt to articulate in terms of cosmic principles clouded his view.

Yet it is possible to specify the types of predicament illustrated in these plays without having to probe the Byronic theology, or theory, of guilt. Marino Faliero has a choice: he can remain in office, an amiable and respected cipher, or try to cleanse the body politic and win real power. Provoked by the Steno insult, he still has a choice. Perhaps such things are best ignored; perhaps the Forty are right to make little of the alleged affront. The Doge is eighty: he has, personally, little to lose, but much to gain for his position. So it is that an old head, a substantial motive and the right pretext combine

to lead him into precipitate action. And however debatable
may be the best way of dealing with the insult, it is truth that
he perceives and acts upon: the truth of his ineffectuality. One
misdemeanour by a member of the Forty alerts the Doge to
the pernicious nature of the whole body. But the attempt to
change the nature of things is doomed from the start: even the
Doge suspected as much. Just before he is led out to execution
on the Giant's Staircase he says to his wife:

> *... there was that in my spirit ever*
> *Which shaped out for itself some great reverse;*
> *The marvel is, it came not until now —*
> *And yet it was foretold me.*

> ANGIOLINA: *How foretold you?*

> DOGE: *Long years ago – so long, they are a doubt*
> *In memory, and yet they live in annals:*
> *When I was in my youth, and served the senate*
> *And signory as podesta and captain*
> *Of the town of Treviso, on a day*
> *Of festival, the sluggish bishop who*
> *Convey'd the Host aroused my rash young anger*
> *By strange delay, and arrogant reply*
> *To my reproof: I raised my hand and smote him. . . .*

Byron always associated self-realization with guilt: to link
oneself with the universe was an act of reverence; to strive
towards a full sense of one's separate identity was apostasy.
Cain was the archetype that brought together Sardanapalus,
royal pansy turned Bellona's bridegroom; Arnold, sport of
nature transformed into Achilles; Doge Foscari, broken, sacked,
but calling for the water that he knows will be poisoned;
Werner, down with his principles, then up with his title;
Manfred, lucubrating on his aspiration to godhead; and Japhet,
transgressing according to the best light he had:

JAPHET: *Father, it cannot be a sin to seek*
To save an earth-born being; and behold,
These are not of the sinful, since they have
The fellowship of angels.

NOAH: *These are they, then,*
Who leave the throne of God, to take them wives
From out the race of Cain; the sons of heaven
Who seek earth's daughters for their beauty?

Self-assertion taints and destroys. If a man repudiates what is forced upon him, he has to take the consequences, whether or not he is being treated justly. Marino Faliero rejects ineffectuality; Sardanapalus, the popular image of himself – astonishing his own troops as well as the enemy; Arnold illicitly rejects his stunted body; Doge Foscari chooses the only positive act left to him, rather than a humiliating dotage; Werner rejects an improper station; Manfred rejects corporeal being; Cain and Japhet, orthodoxy. The gesture is the same, but the motives vary a good deal. Faliero invokes the public good, as does Sardanapalus. Arnold, like Manfred, wishes to cheat for his own ends. Werner cherishes his honour every bit as much as his ambition. Doge Foscari manages a last gesture of defiant pride. The defiance of Cain and Japhet is allegedly humane. But in all these examples, motives and circumstances affect the outcome not at all.

It would not be onerous to extract from Byron's own life the ingredients of such themes. Repudiations, shifts, transformations and heady aspirations were the stock-in-trade of the man who, arriving at the Hotel d'Angleterre in the suburb of Sécheron, in his twenty-eighth year, signed his age as 100. A bit of bravado, of course, but significant bravado. This master of evasion, as lewd as Ovid and with a soul as wrinkled as Gide's was going to be, composed his own *Metamorphoses*. Not for him the truly heroic poem about a lone man surmounting all in order to fulfil an elaborate design of destiny. Not for him the epic hero as raw material for the gods' whims, proving his mettle in adversity. What Byron chose was much more chaotic, much narrower: the futility of the human will in everyday affairs. In some of his plays and romances the lesson is straightforward, given in terms of ethics; in others it is presented symbolically and with supernatural apparatus. It is even possible to argue that Byron's deep sense of the will's ineffectuality led him not only to his theme of the trapped man but also away from a deep respect for human beings. People, this argument would run, were puppets, fit for farce only. And whether they were to be used as mere properties as in *The Deformed Transformed* (unfinished and therefore inscrutable) or as unrespected *personae* in *Beppo* and *Don Juan*, they would exemplify not just a facile fatalism but the principle that self-fulfilment (essence, not existence) is possible only in terms of failure. It is this principle which explains and integrates Byron: the apathy, the disaffected air, the exotic *personae*, the social and literary fulminations, the messianic pose, the melancholy farce and the ludicrous brooding, the early recourse to landscape, the later one to interiors, the cult of magic, the urge to eliminate, the progressive apathy and the final effort to renew, efface or regain his identity. For Byron, a personal identity was both attractive and repulsive: something to be proud of in the teeth of fate, something to obliterate as an earnest of limitation; something at once seductive to the creative man in him, and yet baulking to the pantheist.

It is the romantic who longs to be a soul of indefinite extent but wants to circumscribe the extent in order to savour it. Byron's trapped men cannot escape themselves; each one has a conscience which he is not profligate enough or irresponsible enough to ignore consistently. Each one is romantic enough to enjoy the feeling of being 'self-made', yet is sufficiently aware of the workings of society, destiny and politics to discern his own transgressions. Self-indulgence wars with conscience: 'All a man can betray is his conscience', says Conrad's Razumov in *Under Western Eyes*.

But surely, we are bound to ask, did the communication of such a truism entail all the lavish paraphernalia of Turkish tale, mutiny, incest, beheading, dilapidated castles, Venetian plotters, limp and brisk Assyrians, hunchbacks, swollen rivers, Biblical ventriloquism and Faustian rant? Yes. All this was necessary to Byron both as a poet expressing his deepest feelings and as an acknowledged entertainer. What was instinctive was also good box-office. Indeed, in a sense, Byron's exotic and dramaturgical effects served to objectify vividly; to disguise a subject too familiar to himself. What he eliminated from his spiritual system had to be disclaimed but recognizable; in order to satisfy himself that he had separated it from himself, it must not look so familiar as to be overlooked – as could easily happen. After all, the exotic romance extended back to fable and legend and Byron had a strong sense of the miraculous and the primitive. His writings are exorcisms, and bear many signs – naïve and touching ones – of a yearning familiar to us in many guises: The Fresh Start; 'getting out of himself'; 'breaking new ground'; Adonis myths.

This is not to say that Byron ever articulated the precise nature of this yearning; but determined extrapolators would probably link his deracination with escapism, selfishness, paranoia, inconsistency, and so on. It is not part of this study to pursue such inquiries. It is more to the point to observe that, for Byron, identity was magical and the world was a destructive element. An obsession with self-escape led him naturally to certain themes: escape from a trap, a rôle, a position, an affair, a wife, a reputation; metamorphosis – really transmogrification – into someone else or into a different order of being; contracts with the devil; immersion in action, in poetry, in the exotic; imprisonment; debauchery; bright chatter and foreign travel.

And of course the torrential letter-writing, the menagerie and the changing harem fit into this pattern. Finally he broke free into farce, in which there were no traps. 'Anything goes' is the method of *Don Juan*. The poet usually remains uncommitted, with nothing to escape from or transcend except the strain of his immunity. Even the inveterate evader knows what he is; and to try evading such knowledge is merely to involve oneself all over again with people and objects. *Don Juan* approaches an extreme ideal: an absolute in which Byron has small faith. It is the solution to problems he explored in the romances and plays, and the embodiment of a literary attitude which he could not fully adapt to his life. *Don Juan* and the plays run in parallel. Right up to Missolonghi, the problems intrigued, the solution tempted, and the multiple personality looked for a proper combination of the two.

As literature, the plays are far from perfect; Byron did not often test his powers in them. They communicate a sense of futility – men of stature being fiercely hemmed in by a force which wrecks dignity and stunts responsibility. The straight lines of idealism become inevitably contorted; even the virtuous and the noble fall foul of their own principles. Life cheats but death cannot. These ideas emerge clearly, but too often. There is none of the drama's suggestion of life's movement: the plays are statuesque. Every character is relentlessly ruminative, has no minor emotions, no trivial ideas. If we are to be convinced and disturbed, it is paroxysm that has to do it – paroxysm and proclamation. There is too little of the subtle, irrelevant texture of life; there are too few of those petty but revealing human tricks that keep us sane and the social historians in perpetual business. Everything is made to sound important, almost as if each play contained Station Standing Orders for Good Men Hard Pressed. There is too much elaboration of the crumbling temperament, the stiffening resolve. The main characters – Faliero, Sardanapalus, Foscari, Werner and Manfred

– make an inexorable destiny look flimsy. There are long waits between rounds, and there is too little diversification of the approach to an obvious ending. Most of the secondary characters are the merest figments. There is insufficient use of contrast. The plays proceed like theorems, yet much of the versification is sloppy: syllable count deposes spoken stress; there is too much recourse to speech-spinning devices like anaphora; the language too often lacks trenchancy and wit; much of the verse is careless prose put in layers. There are too few really dramatic images that leap out and epitomize. There is no chatter and too much rant; there is too little play of mono-syllable against polysyllable, of concrete against abstract. The pageant is too insubstantial, too tame, too consciously tricked up in the style of 'plays for study'. And yet for the patient searcher, there is gold – at least, good dramatic pyrites.

To wake us up, for instance, there is verse like a clatter of pans:

> Be not so quick! the honour of the corps
> Which forms the baron's household's unimpeach'd
> From steward to scullion, save in the fair way
> Of peculation; such as in accompts,
> Weights, measures, larder, cellar, buttery,
> Where all men take their prey; as also in
> Postage of letters, gathering of rents,
> Purveying feasts, and understanding with
> The honest trades who furnish noble masters. . . .

This comes from *Werner*, a play not without comic relief, and shows Byron at his cataloguing best. The mouthing bombast catches attention, yet the words seem to impede the ideas' arrival. There is care to supply variety of structure and of movement, but too little attention to a consistent principle of rhythm. Why, in the last four lines, push syllabic count so far as to amputate 'in' and 'with' from their nouns when, elsewhere in the passage, speech-stress lengthens two lines by an extra syllable? If 'with' needs to be exposed to distinguish it from 'of', 'in' certainly does not. The passage is representative of Byron's blank verse style: there is a half-grudging, half-rhapsodical drive at the idea; and disregard reinforces the inconsistency. But in this play, and in *The Deformed Transformed*, Byron at least gets his characters talking in a monstrous version of the colloquial – part Jonson, part Shakespeare, part the Byron of the Letters – which, in appearing to refer to everyday speech, goes much further than the idiom of his other plays. Parody is nearer to life than is the imitation or the dramatically elevated. In the following, Idenstein considers the suitability of a damp room for Stralenheim, who has just been rescued from the river:

> *But then he comes from a much damper place,*
> *So scarcely will catch cold in't, if he be*
> *Still liable to cold – and if not, why*
> *He'll be worse lodged tomorrow. . . .*

This vein of the callous bland is common enough in Shakespeare, and frequent in various applications in Byron – for fun, harsh satire and hysterical hate. Sometimes he pointedly goes through the act of averting his gaze; at other times, he looks on, amused. But there seems to be in his attitude something of the immunity of the gods in Lucretius. Once Byron can regard the person in hand as an object, he writes vividly and secures more attention. About the deformed Arnold in *The Deformed Transformed* he is brilliantly heartless:

> *Were I to taunt a buffalo with this*
> *Cloven foot of thine, or the swift dromedary*
> *With thy sublime of humps, the animals*
> *Would revel in the compliment.*

Mr Punch is using his thick stick on the 'thinginess' of the language. There is a wooden, clumsy sound to this outrageous piece; pathos mingles with bravura, sensitivity with brutishness. We are in the presence of farce. We soar up with 'sublime' and are thumped down by the grotesque, lewd sound of 'hump' – a nice counterpoint of vowels preparatory to the malice of the last line. Jonson's 'Down is too hard, I'll have my beds all stuff'd' belongs with this; but Byron preferred casual farce to such ingenuity, and never achieved Jonson's exquisite inflations of language. Occasionally Byron throws out phrases – 'the helmless dromedary', 'vassals From their scant pallets', 'the lead doth With its greased under-stratum', 'A spur in its halt movements' – which indicate a gift for startling combinations of plain elements. Sophistication goes begging, and the delight in conjunctions that sound uncouth, and look preposterous, prevails:

> . . . *Yesterday he would have given*
> *His lands (if he hath any), and, still dearer,*
> *His sixteen quarterings, for as much fresh air*
> *As would have fill'd a bladder, while he lay*
> *Gurgling and foaming halfway through the window*
> *Of his o'erset and water-logg'd conveyance. . . .*

But Byron has subtler methods. He can work the abstract into a deft mimicry of the tangible:

> . . . *coarse lusts of habitude,*
> *Prurient yet passionless, cold studied lewdness,*
> *Depraving nature's frailty to an art. . . .*
> . . . *but rather lessen,*
> *By mild reciprocal alleviation,*
> *The fatal penalties imposed on life. . . .*

He gains breathtaking advantages merely by setting something ordinary amongst the high-falutin:

> *Shelter'd by the grey parapet from some*
> *Stray bullet of our lansquenets, who might*
> *Practise in the cool twilight.*

This is at least as good as Tourneur or Shirley; and the following is as fine a *trouvaille* as you find anywhere in Byron:

> *I tell thee, be not rash; a golden bridge*
> *Is for a flying enemy.*

It persuades – captures – before its relevance becomes clear. And such, after all, is the function of the dramatic image, even in a dramatic poem. It must epitomize before it can be scrutinized: indeed, scrutiny should be unnecessary, because such an image leaps to the observer's (reader's) need:

> *Ask of the bleeding pelican why she*
> *Hath ripp'd her bosom?*

> *My lord, these are mere fantasies; there are*
> *No eyes in marble.*

> *You* feel *not* – you *go to this butcher-work*
> *As if these high-born men were steers for shambles.* . . .

It is as well to see these images in isolation, for they necessarily isolate themselves from their context. These three preceding come from *Marino Faliero*, which is organized into prodigious leaps from one event to the next. Fortunately, at most of the moments of high intensity – as here at the climaxes of the Doge's first heart-baring to Israel Bertuccio, the conspirator; his first clandestine meeting; and his first qualms about the planned massacre – there is a pregnant image, renewing attentiveness and suffusing what follows. But *Marino Faliero* no less than *The Two Foscari* and *Sardanapalus* starts too slowly and ends too late. Of essentially three-act length, not five, the plots cannot support a viscous magniloquence. In the following passage from *Marino Faliero* the inventive faculty is countering imminent paralysis with frenzied and well-planned exercise:

> I. BER.: *You must come alone.*
> DOGE: *With but my nephew.*

I. BER.: *Not were he your son.*

DOGE: *Wretch! darest thou name my son? He died in arms*
At Sapienza for this faithless state.
Oh! that he were alive, and I in ashes!
Or that he were alive ere I be ashes!
I should not need the dubious aid of strangers.

I. BER.: *Not one of all those strangers whom thou doubtest,*
But will regard thee with a filial feeling,
So that thou keep'st a father's faith with them.

The play is upon the words, not upon our feelings. Byron
gains a meretricious continuity: the use of 'son' and 'strangers'
seems intended to keep things moving in a false reciprocity.
As it happens, the repetition is dramatic, but the language
marks time and suggests speech-spinning. A similar inertia,
prompting the poet into gesticulations, appears as anaphora in
another speech from the same play:

From the hour they made me Doge, the Doge THEY made me –
Farewell the past! I died to all that had been,
Or rather they to me: no friends, no kindnesses,
No privacy of life – all were cut off:
They came not near me, such approach gave umbrage:
They could not love me, such was not the law;
They thwarted me, 'twas the state's policy;
They baffled me, 'twas a patrician's duty;
They wrong'd me, for such was to right the state;
They could not right me, that would give suspicion;
So that I was a slave to my own subjects;
So that I was a foe to my own friends;
Begirt with spies for guards, with robes for power,
With pomp for freedom, gaolers for a council,
Inquisitors for friends, and hell for life!

Now this is a very important speech, intended to carry the
maximum of feeling. True, too, an impassioned person with

some bent for rhetoric tends to resort to anaphora. But so does the poet who wants to accumulate lines; and here the speech feeds on itself. The question is not: is it true to life? but: is its truth to life artfully suggested? To go further: a piece of perfect casting may well entail little or no effort from the actor. But our pleasure at the play is very much bound up with the know-ledge that the whole thing is artificial. And what Byron does, without the stanza form to tax him, is to under-exercise his art. He writes blank verse as if it were an organ of the body, and not an instrument with imposed rules and an arbitrary purpose. Byron the man becomes familiar with the medium and ignores the formalities. He has little conception of art's ventriloquism and too intense a concern with art as sheer self-expression. This is not to say that he cannot project himself into a character, but that he is too interested in such vicarious experience to retain a strong sense of his medium's artificiality. He treats art as if it were a game of identities and not a struggle with objects. So it is that his best writing occurs when he is tussling with a stanza form and writing as himself in unabashed first person. The obvious fusion of these is *Don Juan*.

It is possible to go on from this to say that the sort of thing he writes varies according to fixed conditions. In the first person he derides. If he is *en caractère* – as in the romances, *Childe Harold*, the plays – he usually mistakes art for the exotic, the lifelike, the obedient landscape. Second: even in the first person and tussling with form, he remains naïve about his art. He guards sincerity from feminine rhymes and tries too hard for stunts: the one move is narrow-minded, the other reckless. And third: he wants always to restrict his medium – to make it more and more of a personal thing. In other words, he tried to specialize without developing his taste. He wanted his writing to be as personal as a facial tic, and just as uncontrollable too.

Much of *Don Juan*, *The Deformed Transformed*, *Werner* and *Manfred* comes under the heading of stunt. A stunt travesties our ideas of congruity, and so was dear to Byron. His mystery plays are stunts; his romances are; and his ducal and royal themes seem intended to provoke an exclamation – 'well, of all things!' Even the exotic was a stunt for him: it is true that he did not reconnoitre the Near East with express literary intention; but he found that the exotic enabled him to get away with stunt-themes. *Anything* could happen in Turkey, as his friends must have thought from the outlandish tales he invented about his life there. But once he had seen his way clear to farce, which made the stunt a virtue in its own right, he needed no cover and no pretext; what is exotic in *Don Juan* is therefore either restrained or merely decorative.

But whether the plays are stunts with the time-machine, like *The Deformed Transformed*, or merely specimens of stunted magniloquence, like *Sardanapalus*, there are lovely or pithy passages for the finding. There is a long speech in *Marino Faliero* which perfectly represents Byron when he is fitting himself into a lyrical occasion:

> *The high moon sails upon her beauteous way,*
> *Serenely smoothing o'er the lofty walls*
> *Of those tall piles and sea-girt palaces,*
> *Whose porphyry pillars, and whose costly fronts,*
> *Fraught with the orient spoil of many marbles,*
> *Like altars ranged along the broad canal,*
> *Seem each a trophy of some mighty deed*
> *Rear'd up from out the waters, scarce less strangely*
> *Than those more massy and mysterious giants*
> *Of architecture, those Titanian fabrics,*
> *Which point in Egypt's plains to times that have*
> *No other record. All is gentle: nought*
> *Stirs rudely; but, congenial with the night,*
> *Whatever walks is gliding like a spirit.*
> *The tinklings of some vigilant guitars. . . .*

He is determined to be magniloquent: of course the result is fustian, but is just redeemed by its smoothness and by his eye for objects. The passage could be Rogers, and is anybody; it is built according to the book, with all the right devices. Obviously Byron shared Milton's addiction to the large unit – the paragraph and the self-fed declaration; but he had little of Milton's ability to vary the constructions, to carry many qualifications without losing the pattern of the argument. The most that Byron can attain in this direction is exemplified in the following passage from *Marino Faliero*:

> *I do believe you; and I know you true:*
> *For love, romantic love, which in my youth*
> *I knew to be illusion, and ne'er saw*
> *Lasting, but often fatal, it had been*
> *No lure for me, in my most passionate days,*
> *And could not be so now, did such exist.*
> *But such respect, and mildly paid regard*
> *As a true feeling for your welfare, and*
> *A free compliance with all honest wishes, –*
> *A kindness to your virtues, watchfulness*
> *Not shown, but shadowing o'er such little failings*
> *As youth is apt in, so as not to check*
> *Rashly, but win you from them ere you knew*
> *You had been won, but thought the change your choice;*
> *A pride not in your beauty, but your conduct;*
> *A trust in you; a patriarchal love,*
> *And not a doting homage; friendship, faith, –*
> *Such estimation in your eyes as these*
> *Might claim, I hoped for.*

There is a good deal of dramatic verse inferior to this. Byron achieves a peculiarly apt motion here: constant interpolations in the form of qualification and honest asides give the passage an air of self-interrupting sincerity – a steady pendulum between rehearsed admission and the impulse of the moment. Yet the main drift is never quite lost, largely because as soon as the reader has as much as he can intelligently carry, Byron resorts to parallelism not spread over several lines but based on the single line. The last five lines very gently assist us to earth, and yet add to the information already given. Their function is to calm the reader, to denote the speaker's regained grip on himself after an impassioned outburst. In the same way as a phrase of music repeated *diminuendo*, these last lines attain a dimissory effect which is moving and of which Byron, when he chose, was the master. ('So, we'll go no more a roving' exploits the same device.)

Sufficient to say, then, that Byron was merely too impatient to secure architectonic effects well within his power. But I suggest that the reason underlying the impatience was – in the case of *Marino Faliero*, *The Two Foscari* and *Sardanapalus* especially – boredom with working out the detail of an appealing theme. That is why these three plays suffer from sameness of texture – not an unflagging excellence but the monotony of habit. At least *Werner* and *The Deformed Transformed* have novelties of texture and character blatant enough to keep our attention and sustained enough to have kept Byron reasonably imaginative while composing. *Manfred*, although more of a private pageant-poem than these two, extorts the same kind of attention – the kind we accord to Punch and Judy, *Ubu Roi*, *Bartholomew Fair* and *Waiting for Godot*. All are stunts; but the ideal stunt is short. And Byron's most effective operational unit was the miscellaneous canto's discipline of stanzas. Whatever he laid under contribution could be dismissed without warning; and an argument was as well ended with a flourish in the stanza's last two lines as with a logical clincher.

But in detecting the existence, and in lamenting the failure to operate, of this architectonic gift we should not forget

Byron's mastery of the concise – a mastery essential to the stanza-packer:

> ... *I ne'er*
> *Can see a smile, unless in some broad banquet's*
> *Intoxicating glare, when the buffoons*
> *Have gorged themselves up to equality,*
> *Or I have quaff'd me down to their abasement.*

The verbs 'gorg'd' and 'quaffed' are no idle mannerisms, and will stand up to investigation of the ideas they seem to contrast 'feed up', 'drink up', 'drink down', and so on. This does not assume that Byron intended to be deep; but simply that the contrast is sound enough to bear extrapolation. For he could sharpen the edge of wit with small labour; in the following, he does so by the inclusion of one word, 'magnetic':

> ... *novel perils, like fresh mistresses,*
> *Wear more magnetic aspects. ...*

There are some trenchant exchanges too. Bertuccio declares his motive:

> I. BER.: *Freedom!*
> BEN.: *You are brief, sir.*
> I. BER.: *So my life grows: I*
> *Was bred a soldier, not a senator.*

There is even the old Adam of mock self-consciousness:

> ARN.: *Prithee, peace!*
> *Softly! methinks her lips move, her eyes open!*
> CAES.: *Like stars, no doubt; for that's a metaphor*
> *For Lucifer and Venus.*

Pungency is here too. Sardanapalus, although effete, has a core of common sense, or at least an instinct for what sounds like sense:

> *But what wouldst have? the empire has been founded.*
> *I cannot go on multiplying empires.*

That first line has an almost Thurber-like quality rare in Byron. But whether we are haunted by unusual phrases ('the big rain pattering on the roof') or by Byron's frequent flirtations with aphorism, the fact remains that these plays give us enough of neither. There are flashes of workmanlike economy:

> *Some sacrifices ask'd a single victim,*
> *Great expiations had a hecatomb. . . .*

Occasionally his ear for conversation predominates over his prosy formalities, and the text springs to life briefly:

> *Oh! you wax proud, I see, of your new form:*
> *I'm glad of that. Ungrateful too! That's well;*
> *You improve apace; – two changes in an instant,*
> *And you are old in the world's ways already.*
> *But bear with me. . . .*

Further life accrues from very short and rapid consultations:

> SAL.: *Satraps!*
> BEL.: *My prince!*
> SAL.: *Well met – I sought ye both,*
> *But elsewhere than the palace.*
> ARB.: *Wherefore so?*
> SAL.: *'Tis not the hour.*
> ARB.: *The hour! – what hour?*
> SAL.: *Of midnight.*

But this is everyday device, like the stale epic formulae which Byron appropriated. And a *sortes virgilianae* on the plays is more than unlikely to expose a prodigy, although with their plain and repetitive language, and properly truncated, they might make very suitable pieces for radio.

What is most lacking is a sense of particularity which might tempt the reader to study the imagery. But so much is shallow in this magniloquence meant for casual ears; so much is unsubtle, colourless and passionless. There is more wit than we find in Tennyson the playwright; more energy than in the Johnson of *Irene*; less audacity than in Jonson; less originality than in the Keats of *Otho the Great*, and in all respects less skill than in the Shelley of *The Cenci*. Byron was simply too unimaginative to compose drama: when he wants to brighten things up, he engineers a stunt. He tends to supply factitious energy, to jerk the action along when he himself is bored. The plays really amount to prodigious soliloquies set out as drama; and he seems happiest when he has a long stretch ahead of him into which he can pour himself regardlessly. States of mind intrigue him; events hardly at all.

None of this is surprising in a man devoted to his own moods, a man who released them like wild animals, or pitiable invalids, among the civilized public merely to see what effect they had. Such self-obsession necessarily leads to technical deficiencies such as those already noted. But the themes of the plays really are worth attention, not because they enlighten us about his life, but because they are exhaustive dossiers on special aspects of the human condition. They give no strikingly evident solutions. And this is why I think we are likely to find him readable; for this indolent, wayward, confused and often desperate man was enough of a showman not to try giving answers. If there is any answer, it is in the farce of *Don Juan*. Life, in the plays, remains ineluctable for Doge and hunchback alike; and in striking through fustian, cant and panache to the eternal themes, Byron is at his most serious and sincere. He thought highly of these plays, and so did Goethe. Perhaps they were right. Life is no mere question-and-answer game, and Byron's disdain of packet wisdom is clear from *Don Juan*. Instead, for those who try to think things out, life becomes very often a slowly expanding insight into why the questions are unanswerable anyway. Byron's plays make us think, long-winded as they are. They do not explain or recommend, but illuminate in an uncompromising way the flaws and yearnings of most reflective people. There is a point, after all, at which anguished speculation is seen to be futile, and a steady look at the demons heals better than any exorcizing homily.

Chapter 6

THE SUMMER OF A DORMOUSE

WHAT are we to make of this poet? He gorged on life 'like an Arab or a Boa snake' and poured it back into that unresisting mould, his art. 'All convulsions end with me in rhyme', he said; he restored the peace by resorting like St. Francis to 'the concubine of snow'. The act of writing becomes perfunctory, automatic and often-repeated. He owes allegiance to no political or religious institution; he is mercurial, impatient and arrogant. Yet in his Albany rooms he kept a crucifix; he is reported to have said that he had 'a great mind to believe in Christianity for the mere pleasure of fancying I may be damned'. And there is no doubt that he was much preoccupied with a doctrine of sin and damnation – possibly one of his own contrivance – in which the trapped sinner seeks to transform himself by self-mortification. This man, who boasted of being cunning in his own overthrow, had ample reason to believe in a private devil. Some people said he *was* the devil; certainly he appears to have served himself in that capacity. Perhaps, like Gide, he refused to believe in *the* devil because he could not be sure of hating him. But his writings teem with guilt and the yearning for exculpation; in fact, there is as much concern with original sin as there is in Baudelaire, Eliot and Gide. *Cain, Manfred* and *Heaven and Earth* have much in common with the *Journaux intimes, Ash Wednesday* and *Numquid Et Tu* . . . ? the stretch of his journals that Gide dedicated to Charles du Bos with the epigraph *Numquid et vos seducti estis? (Are you also deceived?)*

All his life he sought some guiding principle: in one sense he found it in Augusta Leigh. He needed a remote symbol of his immortal yearnings – something immune from him. Where he could not worship he lavished kindness; witness his patronage of Nicolo Giraud, 'subject of France, but born in Greece', and of several young Harrovians such as Clare, Wingfield and Dorset. Yet he was more accustomed to tormenting people, to callous emotional experimentation. He ended up treating words in much the same way, which was more of an innovation in English poetry than opening soda-bottles with a poker—and being venomous to actresses—were in manners. It is more interesting to know that he put 'Childe Burun' in his manuscripts than that he wrote offensively to Miss Boyce, the young actress at Drury Lane. But more important than either is the knowledge that he extolled the writings of Mrs Hemans and got scabrous about Keats. His taste in literature was as unreliable as his sexual appetite: he always had a view, just as he was always fancying somebody; but he paid discriminating attention to neither.

The truth is that he had few literary principles, and none that he evolved for himself. Someone or other was always filling him up with cant about 'the unities' and 'irregularity'. He talks of Elizabethan dramatists as if their crime were constipation; and those sanctimonious little bows that he makes in his prefaces have little to do with serious thinking. The sinister thing is that he would accept and apply the literary criteria passed on by such as Matthew Gregory Lewis, author of the freakish and sensual 'Gothic' novel, *The Monk*. Byron as acolyte is a peculiar conception. He never really needed a *Poetics* of any sort; he wrote to get things out of his system, and not according to precept or example. He was as insensitive to form as to people; irresponsibility became eventually his canon; he turned his verses quickly and never bothered his head about keeping up a standard. The romances, coming after the first two cantos of *Childe Harold*, let him down badly. He cared about too many things just momentarily; his worst sins of affectation were passing fancies; his worst utterances were emblems of impatience.

He defies definition – unoriginal but showy; brutal yet capable of great kindness; unprincipled but consistent in his faults; negligent but industrious. Undiscriminating as a critic, nowhere near as well-read as Shelley, he had to make travesty his good. He had eventually to abandon the idols he cherished – the remote Augusta and Goethe, Lord Clare and Nicolo Giraud, and the nearer ones like Rogers, Scott and Moore. Missolonghi typed him as a reluctant hero: it was a gesture of relinquishment, just as in the literary sphere *Don Juan* had been. For once he was on his own, with a large political quest in mind. Similarly, *Don Juan* had exempted him from enlisting either the clichés or the advocacies of other poets: he could make free with the language, and with impunity. If we are to see him in terms of our own times, he can be said to vacillate between Camus's man of stone in *L'Étranger* and Malraux's Garine, the fierce seeker after commitment in *Les Conquérants*. The heirs of Byron's language appear to be Mr Auden, Mr Bemelmans, Mr Betjeman and Mr MacNeice. But the farcical motive seems to have ended where it began. Perhaps no one can be as unresponsive as Byron was. For there is only scattered sympathy in Don Juan; the hero is a drifter, submissive, and a perpetual stranger.

The tenderness of the Haidée idyll and Donna Julia's letter is exceptional: it is unusual in the poem and therefore seems extraordinary – even made over as just another exhibit in the grotesque array. This is not to say that Byron's tenderness was insincere; his attitudes were never absolute. But I do feel that, toying as he was with ideas of alienation from ordinary behaviour and conventional writing, he could not prevent an absurd context from embarrassing passages of tender feeling. Some days he wrote things idyllic or compassionate; most days, he made pugnacious fun; and the day's output, whatever its nature, was pushed into the poem. *Don Juan* lacks not moments of true tenderness but a maintained unity of atmosphere. It is a mixture, not a compound. It gives life's incongruities without art's integration. True, we can enjoy and be moved by such a piece as Donna Julia's letter; but we have to forget where we found it. That is why compilers of anthologies at once fail to show Byron in the round yet serve him in some respects better than he could himself. The letter deserves an undistracted attention:

> *They tell me 'tis decided you depart:*
> *'Tis wise – 'tis well, but not the less a pain;*
> *I have no further claim on your young heart,*
> *Mine is the victim, and would be again:*
> *To love too much has been the only art*
> *I used; – I write in haste. . . .*

Ten lines earlier Donna Inez vows 'To Virgin Mary several pounds of candles'; a stanza or two after the letter ends, the poet is upon us again with a giddy rodomontade:

> *I've got new mythological machinery,*
> *And very handsome supernatural scenery.*

A pity, no doubt; but that is the nature of the poem.

To find a spiritual heir for the Byron of *Don Juan*, we have to look to any literature but the English. Byron's farce with language and his abstention from sympathy appear, curiously enough, to exemplify an outlook which in recent years has gained itself a good deal of theological and literary attention. Marcel, Buber and Brunner have discussed the concept of 'presence': to be involved with one's fellows is the act of being human. And Pavese, in the diary he compiled while contemplating his eventual suicide, suggested that 'Happiness is inseparable from the gift of the self to others. It therefore remains to say that one is happy only when getting out of oneself; that one is happy only when flying off at a tangent.' Hemingway has shown the obverse of this: his sensitives affect the spiritual protection of the 'dumb-ox' pose; the gift of the self is too risky. And Ernst Jünger has propounded an ideal of the mechanistic world in which no one feels: if humanism has failed, then we must abolish it. His ideal, the 'Labourer', is a moronic superman without soul or sensitivity. But perhaps the sanest analysis of 'presence' has come from Arthur Miller: time and again he asserts that man must live by the best light he has, but must not abdicate from human community. Joe Keller in *All My Sons* 'cannot', says Miller, 'admit that he, personally, has any viable connection with his world, his universe or his society'. His personality is divorced from the undertakings in which the body is engaged.

But, equally, and Miller makes this point too, the only thing as fatal as withdrawal of the self is over-concern with and unthinking acceptance of social values. In short, a man has to reconcile presence with absence, combine humanity to others with respect for himself – which Miller's salesman, Willy Loman, conspicuously failed to do. A man must not lose his sense of his own identity; must not, in the phrases of David Riesman, be absolutely 'inner-directed' or absolutely 'other-directed'. The polarities are the extreme romantic agony and the social cipher.

All this bears on Byron's intermittent sense of guilt and his concern with identity. As Byron saw it, excessive concern with oneself was a sin, whether such concern eventuated in disregard of taboo, religious heresy or mere betrayal of one's abilities. To try and escape oneself usually entailed irresponsibility and a disregard of others. The great problem was to be available to others without either losing self-control or accumulating excessive self-esteem. All his characters – in the romances the public liked, and in the plays that Goethe thought only a little below Shakespeare – are groping for a clear moral identity, are all 'refusing the universe', as Malraux would say. They are all in the grip of some web: enforced exile (Conrad, Christian), the rage to avenge (The Giaour), a fraudulent relationship (Selim and Zuleika), a hostile cabal (Doge Faliero, Lara), an unlooked-for rôle (Alp, Sardanapalus), an unjustly denied inheritance or craving (Werner, Hugo), imprisonment (in Chillon), deformity (Arnold), even mortality (Manfred) and original sin (Cain). The web has, in each instance, determined their personality and identity; and when they rebel, the web trips them.

I do not think it has been generally recognized how thoroughly and with what variety he presented such a vital theme. The fretful tergiversations of that spirit *ondoyant et divers* have obstructed approach to the works. 'When he reflects, he is a child': Goethe's verdict is justified; but Byron could see the outlines of the eternal problems, and assess their relevance to himself, even if he could not go into those problems philosophically, ethically and doctrinally. He realized and understood them even if he failed to present a detailed analysis.

He anticipated Lionel Trilling's inquiry into *The Opposing Self*, David Riesman's analysis of *The Lonely Crowd* and Camus's cult of rebellion. Indeed, without frivolity, one might say that *Marino Faliero* anticipates *Death of a Salesman;* both Doge and salesman have identified themselves with a social rôle which slowly destroys them. Both seek to renew their self-respect; both abdicate. And neither sees his predicament in abstract philosophical terms. Throughout, the tone of the protagonists is personal; they know what is happening to them. They do not reflect on this process in general – and both plays suffer from this lack of analysis and deduction. Perhaps Mr Miller will make his characters one day analyze their predicament philosophically. Certainly, from his Introduction to his *Collected Plays*, he seems to know all about that aspect of the action. Byron did not: he was too wrapped up in living.

But what Byron did not define in general terms in his prefaces, he still could recognize. The situations were unmistakable;

and the only ultimate response to them was to turn them into farce. And so the language came to tweak anguish by the nose – to falsify predicaments as meaningfully as Hemingway does. 'Why', Byron asks in *The Age of Bronze*, 'spare men's feelings, when their own are jest?' He took his own hint well – and this one did not come from Horace. The type of response on which *Don Juan* is based emerges from the following note to that poem:

I doubt if 'Laureate' and 'Iscariot' be good rhymes, but must say, as Ben Jonson did to Sylvester, who challenged him to rhyme with –

> *'I, John Sylvester,*
> *Lay with your sister.'*

Jonson answered, – 'I, Ben Jonson, lay with your wife.' Sylvester answered, – 'That is not rhyme.' – 'No', said Ben Jonson; 'but it is *true*'.

The knockabout honesties of *Don Juan* are intended to counter an empirical sadness:

> *The dreary 'Fuimus' of all things human,*
> *Must be declined, while life's thin thread's spun out*
> *Between the gaping heir and gnawing gout.*

Juan is apathetic and passive; he does not battle to survive. And possibly the devastating couplets, which nothing could survive, enact the theme: to survive is to be vitiated by a poison compact of the immutable and the inconsequential. Nothing gets past those couplets: they restore a proper sense of disillusion; they sabotage the purest imagery, the most idyllic sequence and even the cynicism of the maxims themselves. It is a poem of intelligent despair – an inspired gibbering in the lazar-house of the human condition. It inspires, surely, a tremor of horror in every reader. The delicious and demented-looking marionettes wobble through history and society. All is clattering chaos – and the worst demons are the wisdom-packagers, the Rochefoucaulds. It is a poem about ineffectuality; and, as Camus says in *Actuelles II*, there are supposed to be two kinds of ineffectuality – abstention and destructiveness. This poem has both combined: the abstention is from the indestructible human condition – what Camus calls 'history'; and the destructiveness is towards petty wisdoms, which are really attempts to get old without living:

> But heaven must be diverted; its diversion
> Is sometimes truculent – but never mind;
> The world upon the whole is worth the assertion
> (If but for comfort) that all things are kind:
> And that same devilish doctrine of the Persian,
> Of the 'Two Principles', but leaves behind
> As many doubts as any other doctrine
> Has ever puzzled faith withal, or yoked her in.

The poem is all shrugs – 'If but for comfort'. This is cold comfort indeed. But Byron aims to portray, not to argue, a way out; and we are almost always wise to read him for his large effects. Until *Don Juan*, he is not a poet of brilliant texture: he falls by generalized imagery just as he rises by the easily generalized quality of his themes. He had lived widely and intensely enough to discern affiliated ideas. He was keen to go on living like that, and so did not philosophize. He juxtaposed the polarities and left the sparks to themselves. They set fire to the Huysmans, the Hugos, the Nietzsches; but the blaze did nothing to illuminate *Don Juan*. It is now time for the comic Byron to displace his lugubrious avatars. He once meditated like this:

When one subtracts from life infancy (which is vegetation), sleep, eating, and swilling – buttoning and unbuttoning – how much remains of downright existence?

The summer of a dormouse.

THE SUMMER OF A DORMOUSE

If we judge by the wealth of biography, one dormouse made a quite substantial summer. But the 'downright existence' is in the poems and plays, nearly all of which bear on the preoccupations of our own day. It is time, now, for that dormouse to have an Indian summer all of its own.

I

Appendix

A. BYRON'S WRITING HABITS

BYRON always disparaged the poetic vocation and affected the pose of careless scribbler. The following assertions are typical:

> If one's years can't be better employed than in sweating poesy, a man had better be a ditcher. (Letter to Murray, 6 April 1819, Letters and Journals IV, 284.)

> Cut me root and branch; quarter me in the quarterly . . . but don't ask me to alter, for I can't: – I am obstinate and lazy – and there's the truth . . . I told you long ago that the new Cantos were *not* good . . . you may suppress them, if you like, but I can alter nothing. . . . I can neither recast nor replace. . . . I can't piece it together again. I can't cobble. . . . I can't *furbish*. I am like the tyger (in poesy), if I miss my first spring, I go crawling back to my Jungle. There is no second. I can't correct; I can't and I won't. . . . You must take my things as they happen to be. . . . I would rather give them away than hack and hew them. . . . I can't alter. That is not my forte. (Letters to Murray, 12 August 1819; 23 April and 18 November 1820; 19 January 1821; L. & J. IV, 341; V, 16, 120, 225.)

> (Of *Marino Faliero*) I never wrote nor copied *an entire Scene of that play*, without being obliged to *break* off – to *break* a commandment, to obey a woman's, and to forget God's. Remember the drain of this upon a man's heart and brain, to say nothing of his immortal soul. . . . It happened to be the only hour I had in the four and twenty for composition, or reading, and I was obliged to divide even it. (L. & J. V, 90-91.)

> (Of a criticism that *Cain* was too elaborate) What do they mean by *elaborate*? why, *you* know that they were written as fast as I could put pen to paper, and printed from the *original* MSS., and never revised but in the proofs: Look at the dates and the MSS. themselves; whatever faults they have must spring from carelessness, and not from labour; they said the same of *Lara*, which I

wrote while undressing after coming home from balls and masquerades, in the year of revelry 1814. (Letter to Murray, 6 June 1822, L. & J. VI, 76-77.)

But he worked for more than a year at *English Bards and Scotch Reviewers*, enthusiastically expanded parts of *Childe Harold* and *The Bride of Abydos* and kept that 'snake of a poem', *The Giaour*, 'lengthening its rattles'[1] for several months. He laughed off Murray's request for a plan of *Don Juan*; yet he had plans, of a sort, for Juan to do a tour of Europe and for 'A *Satire* on abuses of the present states of Society'. He loathed and shirked proof-reading ('cursed printers' trash'), yet reproved Murray that the printing of *Don Juan*, Cantos III, IV, V was shabbily done. He was always contradicting himself. What, then, are we to make of these lines from *Don Juan*?

> *And therefore I shall open with a line*
> *(Although it cost me half an hour in spinning).*
>
> (Canto I, st. 7, ll. 5-6)

A joke ? A flash of honesty? (He had, in fact, deleted his first attempt at these two lines.) Some facts might help here; and thousands of them have been provided by the Steffan and Pratt Variorum edition of *Don Juan*.[2] Most of the following figures have been taken from that massive and meticulous work of 'dry statistical surprise'.

Byron wrote at extraordinary pace: *The Bride of Abydos* took less than a week, *The Corsair* two, *Lara* four; *Werner* and *The Two Foscari* took a month each; *Heaven and Earth* took a fortnight, as did the last three acts of *Sardanapalus*. The last eleven cantos of *Don Juan* were written in the space of twelve or thirteen months, from April (or May) 1822 to May 1823; the later cantos he composed at immense speed: Canto XI (eleven days), XIII (seven days), XIV (two weeks), XV (three weeks). But what of *English Bards, The Giaour* ('every month for half a year') and, of *Don Juan*, the *Dedication* and Canto I (incomplete after four months), III and IV (which together took three months)? The truth seems to be that he often composed at high speed and corrected at it too. Mr Steffan's summary is worth quoting:

[1] Letter to Murray, 26th August 1813, L. & J. II, 252.
[2] *Don Juan, A Variorum Edition*, ed. T. G. Steffan and W. W. Pratt, 4 vols., Austin, Texas, 1957.

The holographs (he says) of Canto I of *Don Juan* are astonishing
refutations of the generally accepted view not only of Byron's
writing habits but of Byron himself as he wished others to see him.
Most surprising is the evidence that the writing did not come easily
... a very large number of stanzas are almost as much juggled with,
staggered through, pushed all over the page, and blotted as those
about old Angela, the beadsman, Madeline and Porphyro. (See
the Oxford Forman edition of Keat's *The Poetical Works*: 212-29,
where some of the revisions are printed.) . . . Many lines are of
course written straight across the page, one after the other, without interruption or alteration. When he is thus driving steadily
ahead, he may cross a word or the first syllable or letters of a
word, make a change instantly and sail right on. When a line
once written does not satisfy him he usually begins at once to
change it, but sometimes he will get through a stanza, or most of
it, before he goes back to patch or re-form, and occasionally the
differences in handwriting and inking suggest that he waited
until a later session of composition. The changes vary widely in
extent. . . .

But, as Mr Steffan points out, such information must not be
misused:

This is not to say that Byron ever radically reconstructed an
entire canto or any large part of it or that he wrote stanzas, laid
them in a drawer, and came back to furbish them weeks or months
later. In fact there is no evidence on any of the twenty-five
manuscripts of the *Juan* cantos that I have examined that he ever
labored tediously. Nor can it be denied that the handwriting
shows that he was scrawling very fast. But he was also thinking
fast and hard as he wrote, evaluating, rejecting, changing, often
tugging to get words out, taking some care with his verse.
Whether or not any line cost him a half hour in spinning is
impossible to tell, but at least the man who wrote the first draft
manuscripts of the first five cantos did a little mental sweating.
(pp. 104-5.)

Much of Byron's correction seems to have been instantaneous: with
an eye on the clock, another on his London jury (especially Murray
and Gifford), and his vocabulary in a frenzy rolling, he writes down
what another man might discard mentally. He has to get something

out; he has to expel words. He strews his lines with alternatives; he gets down any word that fills the beat; he often 'stammers' – cannot get a stanza started; and turns composition into an inky tumult. He keeps throwing – mud, dice, dart – whatever the metaphor, until something sticks, proves a lucky accident or hits the bull. It is a game of elimination, in both senses of the word. Perhaps that image of the concubine of snow is relevant here; the writing, the self-exhaustion, is performed indiscriminately upon the neutral paper. He is rarely to be found lovingly polishing; but he altered a great deal and, without professing any mystique for his art, did his best to find the right words on the spot. As Mr Steffan testifies:

> . . . proof of the rapidity with which Byron could make his changes and of the way in which revision was an integral part of his composition processes is the large number of alterations made on the run, i.e., in the very act of writing a line across the page. In the matrix stanzas of Canto I (of *Don Juan*) he made 130 changes on the run, 57 of which can be regarded as major revisions, and 73 as minor. (p. 106.)

What we have to do is to revise our own idea of what composition meant to Byron, as distinct from what it meant to, say, Keats and Baudelaire. Byron's corrections are often as hasty as what he first sets down; but *trouvailles* are frequent, and he seems to have to put down *anything* in order to pull them down out of the air. He wakes up the good by writing down what is most probably bad or indifferent. He expects something to turn up; otherwise, heigh-ho, let stand what is there; keep writing, for the very act will bring something out sooner or later. So I think that Peter Quennell is substantially right in saying, 'He had little aptitude for correction or revision'. It is almost as if Byron plays *voyeur* with his own act of writing: he is preternaturally aware of what he is doing, and the spectator and participant are mutually intimate. So he can achieve a truly plastic art. And in this simultaneously critical and creative activity, magical things are sucked out onto the paper. The pen flies, less of a wielded chisel than of a barograph.

Here, finally, are some statistics about *Don Juan*.

(*a*) Only three cantos were published with the same number of stanzas as appeared on Byron's first drafts. 166 stanzas were added, of which 134 went to the first five cantos. Over 60 were added to Canto I. Only 32 were added to the last eleven cantos; IX and XI got most of these.

(b) On 104 occasions, in the whole poem, Byron wrote one or more single word alternatives. 59 of these occasions concerned the final couplet; 47 of the 59, line 8.

(c) Rhyme revision in lines 7–8: rhyme words changed on 88 occasions out of 422 for the whole poem; complete change of rhyme occurred on 218 occasions out of 575 for the whole poem.

(d) There were many more rhyme revisions of line 7 than of complete couplets. In fact line 7 is the most revised line; undergoing 1,211 of the poem's 6,476 revisions (i.e. false starts, deleted and patched fragments, verbal substitutions, rewritten lines, etc.) The next most revised lines are 8 (908) and 6 (838).

(e) Revisions often restore word-order to the colloquial (*the worst deserves* to *deserves the worst*); contract *is it* to *is't: you are* to *you're*; pack the stanza more firmly; restore colloquial usage (*prefers* to *is all for*); tone down earthiness; delete *And* at beginning of lines; often substitute *sage* for *wise*, *deem* for *think*; and introduce feminine rhymes (*learn/earn* to *Herculean/ ultra-Julian*; *time/rhyme* to *Homer/misnomer*) or rhymes simply more bizarre than the original (*worried/buried* to *mob its/ obits*).

B. SPECIMEN REVISIONS

(The words in *italics* are those struck out in the original manuscript.)

English Bards and Scotch Reviewers

1 (MANUSCRIPT FRAGMENT bound in same volume as *British Bards*)
  In these, our times, with daily wonders big,
  A Lettered peer is like a lettered pig;
  Both know their Alphabet, but who, from thence,
  Infers that peers or pigs have manly sense?
  Still less that such should woo the graceful nine;
  Parnassus was not made for lords and swine.

APPENDIX

(Text of the Fifth Edition)

Lords too are Bards: such things at times befall,
And 'tis some praise in Peers to write at all.
Yet, did or Taste or Reason sway the times,
Ah! who would take their titles with their rhymes?

(ll. 719-722)

2 (MS.)

Yet Title's sounding lineage cannot save
Or scrawl or scribbler from an equal grave,
Lamb had his farce but that Patrician name
Failed to preserve the spurious brat from shame.

(Text of the Fifth Edition)

Not that a Title's sounding charm can save
Or scrawl or scribbler from an equal grave;
This Lamb must own, since his patrician name
Failed to preserve the spurious Farce from shame.

(ll. 53-56)

3 (MS. *British Bards* and *E.B. & S.R.* Editions 1-4)

In many marble-covered volumes view
Hayley, in vain attempting something new,
Whether he spin his comedies in rhyme,
Or scrawls as Wood and Barclay walk, 'gainst Time.

(Text of the Fifth Edition)

Behold – Ye Tarts! – one moment spare the text!
Hayley's last work, and worst – until his next;
Whether he spin poor couplets into plays,
Or damn the dead with purgatorial praise,

(ll. 309-312)

Note: *English Bards* grew from 360 lines to 1070; the poem was revised in
83 instances.

Childe Harold: Canto I, Stanza IX

(First Draft, pasted on MS.)

And none did love him though to hall and bower
few could

Haughty he gathered revellers from far and near
An evil smile just bordering on a sneer
He knew them flatterers of the festal hour
Curled on his lip
The heartless Parasites of present cheer
As if
And deemed no mortal wight his peer
Yea! none did love him not his lemmans dear
To gentle Dames still less he could be dear
Were aught But pomp and power alone are Woman's care
But And where these are let no Possessor fear
The sex are slaves Maidens like moths are ever caught by glare
Love shrinks outshone by Mammon's dazzling glare
And Mammon
That Demon wins his (MS. torn) where Angels might despair

(FINAL TEXT)

And none did love him! – though to hall and bower
 He gather'd revellers from far and near,
 He knew them flatt'rers of the festal hour,
 The heartless Parasites of present cheer.
 Yea! none did love him – not his lemans dear –
 But pomp and power alone are Woman's care,
 And where these are light Eros finds a feere;
 Maidens, like moths, are ever caught by glare,
And Mammon wins his way where Seraphs might despair.

Childe Harold: Canto IV, Stanza CXXXIV

(MS.)

     'tis not that now
 And if my voice break forth – *it is not that*
 I shrink from what is suffered – let him speak
    decline upon my
 Who   *humbler in*
 What hath beheld *me quiver on my* brow
  seen my mind's convulsion leave it *blenched or* weak?

APPENDIX

Or *my internal spirit changed or weak*
   found my mind convulsed
             a
But in this page *the* record *which* I seek
               will
              from out the deep
   stands and   *of that remorse*
Shall stand and when that hour shall come and come
Shall come though I be ashes and shall pile heap
It will   *come and wreak*
In fire the measure
The fiery prophecy
The fullness of my
The fullness of my prophecy or heap
The mountain of my curse
Not in the air shall these my words disperse
'*Tis written that an hour of deep remorse*
Though I be ashes *a deep* far hour shall wreak
The fullness Thee   ─ this
The deep prophetic fullness of *my* verse
And pile on human heads the mountain of my curse.

(FINAL TEXT)
    And if my voice break forth, 'tis not that now
      I shrink from what is suffer'd: let him speak
      Who hath beheld decline upon my brow,
      Or seen my mind's convulsion leave it weak;
      But in this page a record will I seek.
      Not in the air shall these my words disperse,
      Though I be ashes; a far hour shall wreak
      The deep prophetic fulness of this verse,
    And pile on human heads the mountain of my curse!

NOTE: Canto I (expanded from 91 to 93 stanzas; underwent 109 revisions;
took two months to write).
    Canto II (80 to 98; 69 revs.; five months).
    Canto III (118 stanzas; 121 revs.; two months).
    Canto IV (127 to 186; 142 revs.; one month).

The Giaour: ll. 68-87

(FIRST DRAFT)

He who hath bent him o'er the dead
Ere the first day of death is fled –
The first dark day of Nothingness
The last of doom and of distress –
Before Corruption's cankering fingers
Hath tinged the hue where Beauty lingers
And marked the soft and settled air ⎞
That dwells with all but Spirit there ⎰ 1
The fixed yet tender lines that speak
Of Peace along the placid cheek
And – but for that sad shrouded eye
That fires not – pleads not – weeps not – now
And but for that pale chilling brow
Whose touch tells of Mortality ⎞
And curdles to the Gazer's heart ⎰ 2
As if to him it could impart
The doom he only looks upon –
Yes but for these and these alone,
A moment – yet – a little hour
We still might doubt the Tyrant's power.

1 (MS. OF FAIR COPY)

And marked the almost dreaming air,
Which speaks the sweet repose that's there.

2 (MS. OF FAIR COPY)

Whose touch thrills with mortality,
And curdles to the gazer's heart.

(TEXT OF SEVENTH AND SUBSEQUENT EDITIONS)

He who hath bent him o'er the dead
Ere the first day of Death is fled,
The first dark day of Nothingness,
The last of Danger and Distress,
(Before Decay's effacing fingers
Have swept the lines where Beauty lingers,)

And marked the mild angelic air,
The rapture of Repose that's there,
The fixed yet tender traits that streak
The languor of the placid cheek,
And – but for that sad shrouded eye,
   That fires not, wins not, weeps not, now,
   And but for that chill, changeless brow,
   Where cold Obstruction's apathy
   Appals the gazing mourner's heart,
   As if to him it could impart
   The doom he dreads, yet dwells upon;
   Yes, but for these and these alone,
   Some moments, aye, one treacherous hour.
   He still might doubt the Tyrant's power;

The Giaour: ll. 1131-1151

(MS.)

Yes Love indeed doth spring from heaven:
If   descend
           be born
A spark of that immortal fire
          eternal
          celestial
To human hearts in mercy given,
   To lift from earth our low desire.
A feeling from the Godhead caught,
To wean from self each sordid thought:
          our
   Devotion sends the soul above,
   But Heaven itself descends to love.
Yet marvel not, if they who love
   This present joy, this future hope
   Which taught them with all ill to cope,
   No more with anguish bravely cope.

(TEXT OF THE SEVENTH AND SUBSEQUENT EDITIONS)
   'Yes, Love indeed is light from heaven;
   A spark of that immortal fire

With angels shared, by Alla given,
   To lift from earth our low desire.
Devotion wafts the mind above,
But Heaven itself descends in Love;
A feeling from the Godhead caught,
To wean from self each sordid thought;
A Ray of Him who formed the whole;
A Glory circling round the soul!
I grant <u>my</u> love imperfect, all
That mortals by the name miscall;
Then deem it evil, what thou wilt;
But say, oh say, <u>hers</u> was not Guilt!
She was my Life's unerring Light:
That quenched – what beam shall break my night?

MS.   (*That quenched, I wandered far in night.*
        'Tis quenched, and I am lost in night.)
      Oh! would it shone to lead me still,
      Although to death or deadliest ill!
      Why marvel ye, if they who lose
        This present joy, this future hope,
      No more with Sorrow meekly cope;

NOTE: Byron expanded *The Giaour* from 407 to 1334 lines.

The Bride of Abydos: ll. 882–9

Variants submitted to Murray and Gifford

(MS.)

  882 The evening beam that smiles the clouds away,
  883 And tints tomorrow with a fancied ray.
                an airy[1]
    And gilds the hope of morning with its ray.
    tints

[1] First draft of a supplementary fragment, to which a note was appended: 'Mr. My. Choose which of the 2 epithets "fancied" or "airy" may be best – or if neither will do – tell me and I will dream another – Yours, B^N.'

And gilds to-morrow's hope with heavenly ray.[1]
And tints tomorrow with prophetic ray![2]

884 Soft as the Mecca Muezzin's strains invite
885 Him who hath journeyed far to join the rite.[3]

884 Blest as the call which from Medina's dome
885 Invites devotion to her Prophet's tomb.

884 Blest as the Muezzin's strain from Mecca's dome
885 Which welcomes Faith to view her Prophet's tomb.

884 Blest – as the Muezzin's strain from Mecca's wall
885 To pilgrims pure and prostrate at his call;

886 Dear as the Melody of better days
     That steals the trembling tear of speechless praise –
     Sweet as his native song to Exile's ears
     Shall sound each tone thy long-loved voice endears.

886 Dear as the melody of better days
     Soft   youthful
887 That steals a silent tear of speechless praise
               the trembling

(TEXT OF THE SEVENTH EDITION)

The evening beam that smiles the clouds away,
And tints to-morrow with prophetic ray!
Blest – as the Muezzin's strain from Mecca's wall
To pilgrims pure and prostrate at his call;
Soft – as the melody of youthful days,
That steals the trembling tear of speechless praise;
Dear – as his native song to Exile's ears,
Shall sound each tone thy long-loved voice endears.

NOTE: The MSS. of *The Bride of Abydos* comprise a bound volume (rough
and fair copies, with sizeable additions) and 32 loose sheets of
additions and emendations.

---

[1] These 2 versions also sent, for Gifford to select which was "best, or
rather *not worst*".

[2] The epithet 'prophetic' was inserted into a revison dated 3 December
1813.

[3] 884-5 were inserted before the quatrain (886-9) on 3 December 1813
and revised three times.

Don Juan: Canto I, 158

(MS.)

1 She ceased & turned upon her pillow; – pale
2 *But beautiful she lay   her   eyes shed tears*
                lays
                lies
                lays,   lies
                            the starting tears
                            and drop the tears
3 *Reluctant past her bright eyes rolled   as a veil*
4 *Like Summer rains through Sunshine*
    As   drop
                        flow fastly
3 *From her bright eyes reluctant rolled the veil*
                            flows as a veil
                            leaps
4 *Of her dishevelled tresses dark appears*
            dark dishevelled tresses
5 *Wooing her cheek   the   dar   black curls strive but fail*
    Contrasting with her cheek   & bosom
                        they
                    her   & strive but fail
2 She lay, her dark eyes flashing through their tears,
3 *As* Like Skies that rain and lighten; as a veil
4 Waved and *oerflowing* her wan cheek appears
                oershading
5 Her *hair* streaming hair – the black curls strive but fail
6 To hide the glossy shoulder which *still* uprears
7 *It's symmetry with*
  In shining
  It's whiteness through them all   with lips
  It's snow through all   *she lay with soft lips*
                    her   lips   sweet lips lay apart
                            ripe lips lie apart
                    her soft lips lie apart,
8 And louder than her breathing beats her heart.

APPENDIX

(FINAL TEXT)

> She ceased, and turn'd upon her pillow; pale
> She lay, her dark eyes flashing through their tears,
> Like skies that rain and lighten; as a veil,
> Waved and o'ershading her wan cheek, appears
> Her streaming hair; the black curls strive, but fail,
> To hide the glossy shoulder, which uprears
> Its snow through all; – her soft lips lie apart,
> And louder than her breathing beats her heart.

Don Juan: Canto IV, 53

(MS.)

> 1 Unless when qualified with thee, Cogniac!
> 2 *But thou   Oh sweet Fury of the fiery* rill
>   Sweet Naïad of the Phlegethontic rill!
> 3 *Makest on the   ner   liver a still worse* attack
>   Ah! why the liver wilt thou thus attack?
> 4 *Besides thy price is something dearer still*
>   And make – like other nymphs – thy lovers ill?
> 5 I would take refuge in weak punch, but R̲a̲c̲k̲
> 6 (In each sense of the word) wheneer I fill
> 7 *My brain and stomach with its*
>   *My brain with blest fumes till my eyes grow dim*
>   *beakers*
>   My *oft replenished* beakers to the brim,
>   mild and midnight
> 8 *Makes* Wakes me next morning with it's Synonime.

(FINAL TEXT)

> Unless when qualified with thee, Cogniac!
> Sweet Naïad of the Phlegethontic rill!
> Ah! why the liver wilt thou thus attack,
> And make, like other nymphs, thy lovers ill?
> I would take refuge in weak punch, but r̲a̲c̲k̲
> (In each sense of the word), whene'er I fill
> My mild and midnight beakers to the brim,
> Wakes me next morning with its synonym.

Don Juan: Canto XII, 37

(MS.)

1 For sometimes they *elect* accept some long pursuer –
2 Worn out with importunity, – or fall
3 (But here *I own* the instances are fewer)
      perhaps
4 To the lot of him who *not* scarce pursued at all –
5 *A drunken Gentleman of Forty's sure* –
  A Hazy Widower turned of Forty's sure –
6 *If he goes after dinner to a ball*
     can hiccup nonsense at a ball
  Whateer astonishment this seems to call
  (If tis not va̲i̲n̲, examples to recall)
7 *To make the very best of*
  For
  To draw *the very best of these fair prizes* –
8 *And show how very useful to advise is.*
  Which shows how very useful good advice is.
7–8 To draw a high prize; now – howeer he got her, I
    See nought more strange in this than t'other Lottery.

(Final Text)

For sometimes they accept some long pursuer,
Worn out with importunity; or fall
(But here perhaps the instances are fewer)
To the lot of him who scarce pursued at all.
A hazy widower turn'd of forty's sure
(If 'tis not vain examples to recall)
To draw a high prize: now, howe'er he got her, I
See nought more strange in this than t'other lottery.

Don Juan: Canto III, 9

(The most abundantly rewritten stanza.)

(MS.)

1 *Life is a play and men*
  All tragedies are finished by a death,

144

APPENDIX

2 All Comedies are ended by a marriage,
3 *For life can go no further*
   These two form the last gasp of Passion's breath
4 *All further is a blank   I won't disparage*
5 *That holy state   but certainly beneath*
6 *The Sun of human things*
3 *These two are levellers, and human breath*
   So   These point the epigram of human breath,
   Or any The future states of both are left to faith,
4 *Though Life and love I like not to disparage*
   The For authors *think* description might disparage
                fear
5 *'Tis strange that poets never try to wreathe* (sic?)
   With eith 'Tis strange that poets of the Catholic faith
6 *Neer go beyond and but seem to dread miscarriage*
7 *So dramas close with death or settlement for life*
   Veiling   Leaving the future states of Love and Life
   The paradise beyond like that of life
8 *And neer describing either*
   To mere conjecture of a devil and or wife
   And don't say much of paradise or wife
5 The worlds to come of both & or fall beneath,
6 And *all both the worlds would blame them for miscarriage*
   And then both worlds would punish their miscarriage –
7 *So leaving both with priest & prayerbook ready,*
   So leaving *Clerg* both *a* each their Priest and prayerbook ready,
8 They say no more of death or of the Lady.

(FINAL TEXT)

     All tragedies are finish'd by a death,
     All comedies are ended by a marriage;
     The future states of both are left to faith,
     For authors fear description might disparage
     The worlds to come of both, or fall beneath,
     And then both worlds would punish their miscarriage;
     So leaving each their priest and prayerbook ready,
     They say no more of Death or of the Lady.

Bibliography

(Place of publication London unless otherwise stated)

1. BYRON'S PRINCIPAL PUBLICATIONS IN VERSE

1806 *Fugitive Pieces*, Newark, private and anonymous

1807 *Poems on Various Occasions*, Newark, private and anonymous
Hours of Idleness, A Series of Poems Original and Translated, Newark

1808 *Poems Original and Translated*, 2nd edition, Newark

1809 *English Bards and Scotch Reviewers*, A Satire (incorporating *The British Bards*, Newark, 1808)

1811 *Hints from Horace* (set up 1811; extracts published 1824 and 1830; full text first published 1831)

1812 *Stanzas on a Lady Weeping*, Morning Chronicle, 7 March (reprinted in *The Corsair*, 2nd edition, 1814)
Childe Harold's Pilgrimage, A Romaunt, Cantos I and II
The Curse of Minerva, private and anonymous; this version next published in 'Philadelphia' (=London?), 1815; (a slightly different text was first published in the New Monthly Magazine, April 1815, as *The Malediction of Minerva, or the Athenian Marble Market* and reprinted under the original title in the 8th edition of *Poems on his Domestic Circumstances*, 1816)
Address spoken at the Opening of Drury Lane Theatre, Morning Chronicle, 12 October (reprinted in *The Genuine Rejected Addresses* presented to Drury Lane Theatre, 1812)

1813 *Waltz*: An Apostrophic Hymn. By Horace Hornem, Esq.
The Giaour, A Fragment of a Turkish Tale
The Bride of Abydos, A Turkish Tale

1814 *The Corsair*, A Tale
Lara, A Tale (with Rogers's *Jacqueline*)

1815 *Hebrew Melodies Ancient and Modern* with Appropriate Symphonies and Accompaniments by I. Braham and I. Nathan

1816 *The Siege of Corinth*, A Poem; *Parisina:* A Poem, anonymous
Fare Thee Well! (three printings privately before publication
in The Champion, 14 April)
A Sketch from Private Life (two printings privately before
publication in The Champion, 14 April)
Poems on his Domestic Circumstances (including *Fare thee Well!*
and *A Sketch from Private Life*; these two poems appeared in
several collections in 1816: see *The Cambridge Bibliography
of English Literature*, Cambridge, 1940, vol. III, pp. 195-6)
Poems
Childe Harold's Pilgrimage, Canto III
The Prisoner of Chillon, and other Poems (including *Darkness:
A Fragment* and *The Dream*)
Monody on the Death of the Right Honourable R. B. Sheridan,
Written at the Request of a Friend, to be Spoken at Drury
Lane

1817 *Manfred*, A Dramatic Poem
The Lament of Tasso

1818 *Beppo*, A Venetian Story, anonymous
Childe Harold's Pilgrimage, Canto IV

1819 *Mazeppa*, A Poem; *Ode on Venice*
Don Juan, Cantos I and II, anonymous

1821 *The Irish Avatar* (private; first published in Thomas Medwin's
Conversations of Lord Byron, 1824)
Marino Faliero, Doge of Venice. An Historical Tragedy in Five
Acts, With Notes. *The Prophecy of Dante*, A Poem
Sardanapalus, A Tragedy. *The Two Foscari*, A Tragedy. *Cain*,
A Mystery
Don Juan, Cantos III-V, anonymous
Heaven and Earth (set up 1821; first published in The Liberal,
No. 2, 1 January 1823; next, Paris, 1823, anonymously)

1822 *The Vision of Judgment*, The Liberal, No. 1, 15 October (next
published Paris, 1822)

1823 *Don Juan*, Cantos VI-VIII; IX-XI; XII-XIV, anonymous
The Age of Bronze; or, Carmen Seculare et Annus haud Mirabilis;
anonymous
The Island, or, Christian and his Comrades

The Blues, A Literary Eclogue, The Liberal, No. 3, 26 April
(reprinted in *Works*, 1831)

Morgante Maggiore di Messer Luigi Pulci (verse translation),
The Liberal, No. 4, 30 July (reprinted in *Works*, 1824)

Werner: A Tragedy

1824 *Don Juan*, Cantos XV and XVI, anonymous

The Deformed Transformed, A Drama

On this day I complete my 36th year, Morning Chronicle,
29 October; reprinted in *Works*, 1831)

1832 *Lines on hearing that Lady Byron was ill*, New Monthly
Magazine, August

1833 Dedication to *Don Juan*

1898-1904 *The Works*, 13 vols. (Poetry ed. E. H. Coleridge, 7 vols;
Letters and Journals ed. R. H. Prothero, 6 vols.)

1905 *The Poetical Works*, 1 vol., ed. with Memoir by E. H. Coleridge

1957 *Don Juan: A Variorum Edition* ed. T. G. Steffan and W. W.
Pratt, 4 vols., Austin, Texas

2. SOME CRITICAL WRITINGS MAINLY ON BYRON AS POET

Hazlitt, William, *Lectures on the English Poets*, 1818

——, *The Spirit of the Age*, 1825

Watts, A. A., 'Lord Byron's Plagiarisms', *Literary Gazette*, 24
February-31 March 1821

Hugo, Victor, 'Sur George Gordon, Lord Byron', *La Muse Française*,
15 June 1824

Scott, Sir Walter, 'The Death of Lord Byron', *Edinburgh Weekly
Journal*, 19 May 1824 (reprinted in *Miscellaneous Prose Works*,
vol. I, Edinburgh, 1841)

Styles, John, *Lord Byron's Works Viewed in Connexion with Christianity and the Obligations of Social Life*, 1824

(Phillips, W.) 'A Review of the Character and Writings of Lord
Byron', *Atlantic Monthly*, October 1825

BIBLIOGRAPHY

'Stendhal' (Henri Beyle) 'Lord Byron en Italie et France', *Revue de Paris*, March 1830

Macaulay, T. B. Lord, 'Lord Byron', *Edinburgh Review*, June 1831 (reprinted in *Critical and Miscellaneous Works*, vol. I, Philadelphia, 1841)

'Sand, George' (A. A. L. Dudevant) 'Essai sur le Drame Fantastique: Goethe, Byron, Mickiewicz', *Revue des Deux Mondes*, 1 December 1839) reprinted in *Autour de la Table*, Paris, 1862)

Jeffrey, Francis, Lord, *Contributions to the Edinburgh Review*, 4 vols. 1844

Richardson, D. L., *Literary Recreations*, 1852 ('Byron's Opinion of Pope')

Kingsley, Charles, 'Thoughts on Shelley and Byron', *Fraser's Magazine*, November 1853 (reprinted in *Miscellanies*, I, 1859)

Hannay, J., *Satire and Satirists*, 1854

Swinburne, A. C., *Essays and Studies*, 1875

——, 'Wordsworth and Byron', *The Nineteenth Century*, April-May 1884 (reprinted in *Miscellanies*, 1886)

Nichol, J., *Byron*, 1880

Ruskin, John, 'Fiction, Fair and Foul', *The Nineteenth Century*, September 1880 (reprinted in *Works*, ed. Cook and Wedderburn, vol. XXXIV)

Jowett, B., *Byron*, Oxford, 1884 (privately printed)

'Gerard, William' (William Gerard Smith), *Byron Re-studied in his Dramas*, 1886

Arnold, Matthew, 'Byron', *Essays in Criticism*, series 2, 1888

Henley, W. E., *Views and Reviews*, 1890

Phillips, Stephen, 'The Poetry of Byron', *Cornhill Magazine*, January 1898

'Rutherford, Mark' (W. H. White), *Pages from a Journal*, 1900 ('The Morality of Byron's Poetry')

Symons, Arthur, *The Romantic Movement in English Poetry*, 1909

Chew, Samuel C., *The Dramas of Lord Byron*, Göttingen, 1915

Briscoe, W. A., (ed.) *Byron the Poet*, 1924

Chambers, R. W., *Ruskin (and Others) on Byron*: 1925 (English Association Lecture)

Drinkwater, John, *The Pilgrim of Eternity: Byron – A Conflict*, 1925

Ker, W. P., *Collected Essays*, 2 vols., 1925

Robertson, J. G., 'Goethe and Byron', Publications of the English Goethe Society, N.S. II, 1925

Dargan, E. P., 'Byron's Fame in France', *Virginia Quarterly*, II, 1926

du Bos, Charles, *Byron et le besoin de la fatalité:* Paris, 1929 (English translation by E. C. Mayne, 1932)

Praz, Mario, *The Romantic Agony*, 1933

Quennell, Peter, *Byron: the Years of Fame*, 1935
——, *Byron in Italy*, 1941

Leavis, F. R., 'Byron's Satire' (*Revaluation*), 1936

Dobrée, Bonamy (ed.), *From Anne to Victoria*, 1937 (essay on Byron by T. S. Eliot)

Marjarum, E. W., *Byron as Skeptic and Believer*, Princeton, N.J., 1938

Nicolson, Sir Harold, *The Poetry of Byron*, 1943 (English Association Presidential Address)

Boyd E. F., *Byron's 'Don Juan': A Critical Study*, New Brunswick, 1945

Gray, D., *The Life and Work of Lord Byron*, Nottingham, 1945

Russell, Bertrand, *A History of Western Philosophy*, 1946 (pp. 774-781)

Butler, E. M., *Byron and Goethe*, 1951

Read, Herbert Sir, *Byron*, 1951 ('Writers and Their Work': No.10)

Knight, G. Wilson, *Lord Byron: Christian Virtues*, 1952
——, *Byron's Dramatic Prose:* 1953 (University of Nottingham Byron Foundation Lecture)

Robson, W. W., *Byron as Poet*, Oxford, 1957 (Chatterton Lecture, British Academy)

Escarpit, Robert, *Lord Byron*, 2 vols., Paris, 1958

Marchand, Leslie A., *Byron, A Biography*, 3 vols., 1958

Wain, John, 'Byron: The Search for Identity', *The London Magazine*, July 1958

QUOTATIONS

(From poems and plays)

INDEX

INDEX